250 Instant Pot Duo Crisp Air Fryer Cookbook

Affordable, Easy and Delicious Instant Pot Air Fryer Crisp Recipes for Beginners.

by
Noah White

Table of Contents

Introduction

The Instant Pot is a popular cooking appliance. It can perform several cooking functions and make your life easier. You can fry, bake, grill, and roast your food in the Instant Pot. This cooking appliance has got even better with the Instant Pot air fryer crisp. With this new appliance, you can even air fry your food by just changing the lid.

The design of this cooking appliance is simple, effective, and not complex at all. The pressure cooker and air fryer lid are easily locked in their place without much hassle. Air fryers are very popular these days. However, without good recipes, this appliance is useless. This cookbook will help you make the best of your Instant Pot air fryer crisp. This one cookbook has numerous mouth-watering recipes that can help you cook your food with very little oil or absolutely no oil. If you want to live a life full of energy, lose weight, and stay healthy, then this cookbook is for you.

Let's take a look at what this cookbook offers you:

- o 250 super yummy and healthy recipes for breakfast, vegetarians, vegans, poultry, fish and seafood, beef, lamb, pork, snacks and appetizers, and desserts.

- o This book will help you eat oil-free meals, lose weight and stay healthy

- o If weight loss is your goal, then this cookbook is for you.

- o If you have a job or are a busy mom, then this cookbook helps you with many quick recipes using the Instant Pot air fryer crisp.

With your Instant Pot air fryer crisp, you get the benefit of two cooking appliance in one! So, what are you waiting for? Don't wait another second to get this amazing cookbook now. Just Click "Add to Cart" and start your new happy life today!

Mini Turkey Pies

Cook time: 10 minutes |Serves: 8| Per serving: Calories 47; Carbs 3g; Fat 3g; Protein 2g

Ingredients:

- Filo pastry – 8 slices
- Shredded turkey – 1.76 oz.
- Egg – 1, beaten
- Coconut milk – 1.60 ml
- Whole milk – 1.6 oz.
- Tomato sauce – 7 oz.
- Turkey stock – 1 oz.
- Oregano – 1 tsp.
- Coriander – 1 tbsp.
- Salt and pepper to taste

Directions:

Place the wet ingredients into a bowl apart from the egg and mix well. Add the turkey and seasoning and mix well. Set aside. Line little pie cases with a bit of flour and then line with the filo pastry. Aim for one sheet of filo for each pie. Add the mixture to each mini pie pot and fill about ¾. Cover the top with the remaining pastry and then brush the egg along the top. Place them into the air fryer basket. Close and cook for 10 minutes at 350F. Serve.

Sweet and Smokey Chickpeas

Cook time: 16 minutes |Serves: 4| Per serving: Calories 410; Carbs 69g; Fat 6g; Protein 20g

Ingredients:

- ○ Chickpeas – 1 (15-ounce) can
- ○ Aquafaba from chickpeas – 2 tbsps.
- ○ Maple syrup – 1 tbsp.
- ○ Smoked paprika – 2 tsps.
- ○ Garlic powder - 1 ½ tsps.
- ○ Sea salt – ½ tsp.

Directions:

Drain the chickpeas while reserving aquafaba obtained. Do not rinse chickpeas. Add chickpeas to the air fryer basket and shake to a single layer. Choose the air fryer function and close the lid. Air fry at 390F for 8 minutes. Meanwhile, whisk together 2 tbsps. of aquafaba, maple syrup, smoked paprika, garlic powder, and salt in a bowl. When cooked, add the chickpeas in this mixture and coat. Return the coated chickpeas with the sauce to the air fryer basket and air fryer at 390F for 5 minutes more. Shake the basket and cook again for 3 to 5 minutes. Serve.

Turkey Fajitas Platter

Cook time: 20 minutes |Serves: 3| Per serving: 647; Carbs 44g; Fat 39g; Protein 30g

Ingredients:

- ○ Tortilla wraps – 6
- ○ Leftover turkey breast – 3.5 oz.
- ○ Avocado – 1, chopped
- ○ Bell peppers – 3, chopped
- ○ Small red onions – ½
- ○ Soft cheese – 5 tbsps.
- ○ Cajun spice – 3 tbsps.
- ○ Mexican seasoning – 2 tbsps.
- ○ Cumin – 1 tsp.

- o Salt and pepper to taste

- o Fresh coriander – ½ cup

Directions:

Slice the vegetables and chop the turkey breast into small chunks. Place everything in a bowl and mix. Place in silver foil and them place all of them in the air fryer basket. Close the lid. Cook on Air Fry more at 390F for 20 minutes. Serve.

Kale Crips
Cook time: 10 minutes |Serves: 2| Per serving: Calories 75.4; Carbs 2.3g; Fat 7g; Protein 0.8g

Ingredients:

- o Kale – 1 bunch, stems and ribs removed; leaves chopped

- o Olive oil – 2 tbsps.

- o Salt and pepper to taste

Directions:

Preheat the air fryer to 390F. In a bowl, mix kale, olive oil, salt and pepper. Bake the kale mix in the air fryer in batches, about 5 minutes each time. Serve.

Air Fryer Granola
Cook time: 15 minutes |Serves: 8| Per serving: Calories 351; Carbs 38g; Fat 19g; Protein 7g

Ingredients:

- o Rolled oats – 2 cups

- o Toasted wheat germ – ½ cup

- o Dried cherries – ¼ cup

- o Dried cranberries – 1/8 cup

- o Dried blueberries – ¼ cup

- o Pepitas – 1/8 cup

- o Sunflower seeds – 1/8 cup

- o Flaxseed – 1 tbsp.

- o Chopped pecans – 1/8 cup

- o Chopped almond – 1/8 cup

- o Chopped walnuts – 1/8 cup

- o Chopped hazelnuts – 1/8 cup

- o Honey – 2 tbsps.

- o Vanilla extract – ½ tsp.

- o Maple syrup – ¼ cup

- o Olive oil – 6 tbsps.

- o Ground cinnamon – ½ tsp.

- o Ground cloves – 1/8 tsp.

Directions:

Combine all the dry ingredients in a bowl. Mix the honey with oil and maple syrup. Mix the syrup mix with the dry ingredients. Preheat the air fryer at 350F. Add the mix to the air fryer basket and cook for 15 minutes. Stirring after every 5 minutes. Cool and serve.

Egg Frittata

Cook time: 15 minutes |Serves: 2 | Per serving: Calories 227; Carbs 6g; Fat 15g; Protein 17g

Ingredients:

- o Eggs – 4

- o Milk – ½ cup

- o Green onions – 2 chopped

- o Baby Bella mushrooms – ¼ cup, chopped

- o Spinach – ¼ cup, chopped

- o Red bell pepper – ¼ cup, chopped

- o Cheddar cheese – ¼ cup

- o Salt – ½ tsp.

- o Black pepper – ½ tsp.

- o   Dash of hot sauce

- o   Butter to grease the pan

Directions:

Grease a pan and set aside. Whisk the eggs and milk in a bowl. Stir in green onions, mushrooms, salt, black pepper, spinach, red bell pepper, cheddar cheese and hot sauce. Pour the egg mixture into a greased pan. Place in the air fryer basket and close. Cook on 360F for 15 to 18 minutes. Serve.

Air Fried Mac and Cheese
Cook time: 35 minutes |Serves: 4| Per serving: Calories 291; Carbs 18.8g; Fat 16.5g; Protein 16.9g

Ingredients:

- o   Elbow macaroni – 1 cup

- o   Broccoli or cauliflower – ½ cup, equal size small florets

- o   Warmed milk – ½ cup

- o   Grated cheddar cheese – 1 ½ cups

- o   Salt and pepper

- o   Parmesan cheese – 1 tbsp. grated

Directions:

Preheat the air fryer at 390F. Boil some water over high heat. Lower heat and add macaroni and vegetables. Simmer for 7 to 10 minutes or until macaroni is al dente. Drain the vegetables and pasta and place them to the pot. Add cheddar cheese and milk and mix. Season with salt and pepper. Pour pasta mixture into an ovenproof dish. Then sprinkle the parmesan cheese. Bake in the air fryer basket at 350F for 15 minutes. Allow it to sit for 5 to 10 minutes in the air fryer. Serve.

Steak Kebabs
Cook time: 12 minutes |Serves: 4| Per serving: Calories 310; Carbs 9g; Fat 18g; Protein 28g

Ingredients:

- o   Sirloin steak – 1 lb. cut into 1-inch chunks

- o   Olive oil – ¼ cup

- o   Soy sauce – ¼ cup

- o   Garlic – 1 tbsp. minced

- o Brown sugar – 1 tsp.

- o Ground cumin – ½ tsp.

- o Black pepper – ¼ tsp.

- o Baby Bella mushrooms – 8 oz. stem removed

- o Red onion – 1, chopped

- o Green Bell pepper – 1, chopped

- o Salt and pepper to taste

Directions:

Preheat the air fryer to 390F. Mix soy sauce, garlic, cumin, salt, steak, olive oil, and black pepper. Marinate for 30 minutes. Then place the marinated meat, mushrooms, green pepper, and red onion in the air fryer basket. Cover and cook for 10 to 12 minutes. Flip once at the halfway mark.

Hard-Boiled Eggs
Cook time: 15 minutes |Serves: 3| Per serving: Calories 56; Carbs 0g; Fat 4g; Protein 5g

Ingredients:

- o 6 eggs

Directions:

Preheat the air fryer at 390F. Then place the eggs in the air fryer basket and close. Air fry for 15 minutes at 300F. Then remove the eggs and place them in icy water. Serve.

Hot Dogs
Cook time: 8 minutes |Serves: 6| Per serving: Calories 228; Carbs 30g; Fat 8g; Protein 9g

Ingredients:

- o Hot dogs – 6

- o Hot dog buns - 6

Directions:

Place the hot dogs in the air fryer basket and close the lid. Cook at 400F for 4 to 6 minutes. Then remove and put them in the buns. Cook again for 2 minutes at 400F. Serve.

Air-Fried Scotch Eggs

Cook time:15 minutes| Serves:5| Per serving: Calories 407; Carbs 10.65g; Fat 29.44g; Protein 24.91g

Ingredients:

- o   Egg – 1 beaten
- o   Bulk sausage – 1 lb. uncooked
- o   Hard-boiled eggs – 5, peeled
- o   Hot sauce
- o   Oil spray for coating
- o   Almond flour – 1 cup

Directions:

Divide the sausage into six equal parts and flatten to make a 4-inch wide patty. Lay boiled eggs in the center and wrap the patty around it. Repeat. Dip each sausage-wrapped patty in the beaten egg and then into the breading for coating. Spray all sides evenly with oil. Place in the air fryer basket and cover. Cook at 400F for 12 to 16 minutes. Turn once at the halfway mark. Once done, cut in half and serve with hot sauce.

Mac and Cheese

Cook time: 25 minutes |Serves: 6| Per serving: Calories 680; Carbs 22g; Fat 56g; Protein 22g

Ingredients:

- o   Macaroni - 2 ½ cups
- o   Sharp cheddar - 2 2/3 cups, grated
- o   Breadcrumbs – 1 cup
- o   Chicken stock - 2 cups
- o   Heavy cream -1 ¼ cups
- o   Parmesan cheese – 1/3 cup, shredded
- o   Butter – 8 tbsps. melted and divided
- o   Garlic powder – ¼ tsp.
- o   Salt and pepper to taste

Directions:

Place the inner pot in the Instant Pot and add the chicken broth. Add the heavy cream, four tbsps. of butter and macaroni. Pressure cook for 5 minutes or until al dente. Combine the breadcrumbs with the remaining butter in a bowl. Quick-release the pressure and stir in two cups of sharp cheddar. Top with the remaining 2/3 cup of sharp cheddar, 1/3 cup parmesan cheese and breadcrumb mixture. Air fry at 400F for 5 minutes or until browned. Serve.

Air Fryer Cheeseburgers

Cook time: 8 minutes |Serves: 4 | Per serving: Calories 413; Carbs 7g; Fat 25.4g; Protein 4g

Ingredients:

- o   Ground beef – 1 pound
- o   Soy sauce – 1 tbsp. low-sodium
- o   Garlic – 2 cloves, chopped
- o   American cheese – 4 slices
- o   Hamburger buns – 4
- o   Mayonnaise – 4 tbsps.
- o   Red onion – ½ cup, sliced
- o   Salt – ½ tsp.
- o   Ground black pepper – ½ tsp.
- o   Lettuce – 2 ounces

Directions:

Combine soy sauce, garlic, and beef in a bowl. Make 4 patties. Then season with salt and pepper. Place in the air fryer basket and cover. Cook at 380F for 8 minutes on Air Fryer mode. After 4 minutes, open and top it with a cheese sliced and cook. Arrange the burgers and serve.

Mozzarella Sticks

Cook time: 8 minutes |Serves: 6| Per serving: Calories 56; Carbs 7g; Fat 1.9g; Protein 2g

Ingredients:

- o   Mozzarella sticks – 6 (8-ounces) each
- o   Panko breadcrumbs - 1 cup
- o   Eggs – 2

- o   All-purpose flour – 3 tbsps.

- o   Crushed black pepper – ½ tsp.

- o   Salt – ½ tsp.

- o   Marinara sauce – ¼ cup

Directions:

Freeze the mozzarella in the freezer. Beat the eggs in a bowl. Place the breadcrumbs in another bowl. Keep the all-purpose flour in another bowl. Dredge the mozzarella sticks in the flour and shake off excess. Then dip in the beaten egg and then dredge in the panko bread crumbs. Lastly, dip in the egg liquid. Line the air fryer basket with parchment and place in the mozzarella sticks. Cover and cook at 400F for 8 minutes. Serve with marinara sauce.

Sweet Potato Hash
Cook time: 15 minutes |Serves: 6| Per serving: Calories 191; Carbs 31.4g; Fat 6g; Protein 3.7g

Ingredients:

- o   Large sweet potato – 2, chopped

- o   Bacon – 2 slices

- o   Olive oil – 2 tbsps.

- o   Paprika – 1 tbsp. smoked

- o   Dried dill weed – 1 tsp.

- o   Ground black pepper – 1 tsp.

- o   Salt – 1 tsp.

Directions:

Preheat the air fryer at 390F for 5 minutes. In a bowl, add everything and mix. Place in the air fryer. Cook at 390F for 12 minutes. Stir the potatoes 2 to 3 times during the cooking process. Serve.

Breakfast Frittata
Cook time: 18 minutes |Serves: 2| Per serving: Calories 380; Carbs 2.9g; Fat 27.4g; Protein 31.2g

Ingredients:

- o   Eggs – 4, beaten

- o   Breakfast sausage – ¼ pound, cooked and crumbled

- o   Red bell pepper – 2 tbsps. chopped

- o   Cheddar cheese – ½ cup, grated

- o   Green onion – 1, chopped

- o   Ground cayenne pepper – ¼ tsp.

- o   Salt to taste and cooking spray

Directions:

In a bowl, combine the egg, sausage, grated cheddar cheese, onion, salt, and cayenne pepper. Mix well. Grease the air fryer basket with cooking spray. Pour the egg mix into the basket and cover. Close the lid and cook at 350F for 18 minutes. Serve.

Sausage Patties

Cook time: 10 minutes |Serves: 4 | Per serving: Calories 145; Carbs 0.7g; Fat 9g; Protein 14.1g

Ingredients:

- o   Sausage patties – 1 (12-ounce) packet

- o   Non-stick cooking spray

Directions:

Grease the air fryer basket and place in the patties. Do not overcrowd the basket. Spray some cooking oil on top of the patties. Cover and cook at 400F for 5 minutes. Serve.

Ham and Egg Toast Cups

Cook time: 15 minutes |Serves: 4| Per serving: Calories 380; Carbs 5g; Fat 30g; Protein 21g

Ingredients:

- o   Toast slices – 8

- o   Ham slices – 2, cut into 8 strips

- o   Eggs – 4

- o   Butter – 2 ounces

- o   Ground black pepper and salt to taste

- o   Cheese – 4 ounces

Directions:

Grease 4 ramekins with butter. With a rolling pin, flatten the toast to the maximum level. Now line each ramekin with 2 toast slices. Then line each ramekin with 2 ham strips. Now on each toast cup, crack one egg per toast cup. Season with salt and pepper. Then place cubed cheese. Place the cups in the air fryer basket and cook at 320F for 15 minutes. Serve.

Air Fryer Omelet
Cook time: 8 minutes |Serves: 2| Per serving: Calories 355; Carbs 9g; Fat 24.5g; Protein 25g

Ingredients:

- Eggs – 2
- Milk – ¼ cup
- Green onions – ¼ cup, diced
- Bell pepper – 2, chopped
- Mushrooms – ¼ cup, chopped
- Ham – 4 ounces, chopped
- Breakfast seasoning – 1 tsp.
- Cheese – ¼ cup, grated
- Salt to taste
- Oil – 1 tbsp.

Directions:

Mix milk and egg in a bowl. Season with salt. Put all the veg and ham into the mix and mix. Pour the mix into a pan. Place the pan in the air fryer basket and cover. Cook at 350F for 8 minutes. After 4 minutes, open the lid and sprinkle the breakfast seasoning and cheese. Cover and finish cooking. Serve.

Healthy Breakfast Bake
Cook time: 25 minutes |Serves: 2| Per serving: Calories 173; Carbs 14g; Fat 9g; Protein 9g

Ingredients:

- Wholegrain bread – 1 slice, torn into pieces
- Eggs - 4

- Baby spinach – 1 ½ cups

- Shredded cheddar cheese – ¼ cup plus 2 tbsps. divided

- Bell pepper – ½ cup, diced

- Milk – 2 tbsps.

- Hot sauce – 1 tsp.

- Salt – ½ tsp.

Directions:

Preheat the air fryer to 250F. Grease a souffle dish with cooking spray. Beat the eggs, hot sauce, milk, and salt in a bowl. Gently fold in the spinach, ¼ cup cheddar, bread pieces, and bell pepper. Pour the egg mixture into a souffle dish and place in the air fryer basket. Cook at 250F for 20 minutes. Sprinkle the top with remaining cheese and cook 5 minutes more. Serve.

Bacon and Croissant

Cook time: 10 minutes |Serves: 2 | Per serving: Calories 643; Carbs 57g; Fat 39g; Protein 16g

Ingredients:

- Thick-cut bacon – 4 pieces

- Croissants – 2, sliced

- Eggs – 2

- Butter – 1 tbsp.

For the sauce

- Ketchup – ½ cup
- Apple cider vinegar – 2 tbsps.
- Brown sugar – 1 tbsp.
- Molasses – 1 tbsp.
- Worcestershire sauce – ½ tbsp.
- Onion powder – ¼ tsp.
- Mustard powder – ¼ tsp.
- Liquid smoke – ¼ tsp.

Directions:

Preheat the air fryer to 390F. Mix all the sauce ingredients in a saucepan and heat until sauce thickens slightly. Place the bacon cuts flat on a tray and brush them with sauce on one side. Transfer to the air fryer basket with the brushed side up. Cook for 5 minutes then flip. Brush the other side with sauce and cook for 5 minutes more. Melt the butter in a pan and fry the eggs. Then place the eggs at the bottom of each croissant. Top them with two bacon slices each and close the croissant top. Serve.

Air-Fried French Toast Sticks

Cook time: 12 minutes |Serves: 2| Per serving: Calories 163; Carbs 2g; Fat 15g; Protein 5g

Ingredients:

- ○ Sandwich bread – 4 pieces
- ○ Softened butter – 2 tbsps.
- ○ Eggs – 2, beaten
- ○ Ground cloves – 1 pinch
- ○ Cinnamon – 1 pinch
- ○ Nutmeg – 1 pinch
- ○ Salt – 1 pinch
- ○ Maple syrup for garnish

Directions:

Preheat the air fryer to 350F. Beat the cinnamon, eggs, nutmeg, cloves, and salt in a bowl. Butter both sides of the bread slices and cut them into strips. Dredge each bread strip in the egg mixture. Arrange them in the air fryer basket. Cook for 2 minutes, then spray with cooking spray and flip. Cook the other side for 4 minutes. Careful not to burn. Drizzle with maple syrup and serve.

Ranchero Wraps

Cook time: 8 minutes |Serves: 2| Per serving: Calories 290; Carbs 26g; Fat 14g; Protein 15g

Ingredients:

- ○ Egg scramble – 2 servings
- ○ Flour tortillas – 2-large
- ○ Corn tortillas – 2-small
- ○ Pinto beans – 1/3 cup, cooked
- ○ Ranchero sauce – ½ cup
- ○ Avocado – ½, peeled and sliced

o   Fresh jalapenos – 2, stemmed and sliced

Directions:

Assemble the large tortillas on a work surface. Arrange the crunch wraps by stacking the following ingredients in order: egg scramble, jalapeno, ranchero sauce, corn tortillas, avocado, and pinto beans. Fold to seal completely. Place one crunch wrap in the air fryer basket and cook at 350F for 6 minutes. Repeat and serve.

Garlic Bread
Cook time: 5 minutes |Serves: 4| Per serving: Calories 288; Carbs 35g; Fat 12g; Protein 10g

Ingredients:

o   Ciabatta – 4 slices

o   Parmesan – ¼ cup, grated

o   Salted butter – 1 tbsp.

o   Garlic – 3 cloves, crushed

o   Dried parsley to taste

Directions:

Preheat the air fryer to 360F. Melt the butter in a microwave. Add the garlic, cheese, and dried parsley to the bowl of butter. Spread the garlic mixture to both sides of ciabatta slices. Cook for 5 minutes. Serve.

Shrimp and Rice Breakfast Frittata
Cook time: 15 minutes |Serves: 4| Per serving: Calories 226; Carbs 19g; Fat 9g; Protein 16g

Ingredients:

o   Eggs – 4

o   Pinch salt

o   Dried basil – ½ tsp.

o   Cooked rice – ½ cup

o   Chopped cooked shrimp – ½ cup

o   Baby spinach – ½ cup

- o   Grated cheese – ½ cup

Directions:

Beat the eggs with salt and basil until frothy in a bowl. Spray a pan with nonstick cooking spray. Combine the spinach, shrimp, and rice in the prepared pan. Pour the eggs in and sprinkle with the cheese. Bake at 320F until frittata is puffed and golden brown, about 14 to 18 minutes. Serve.

Omelette in Bread Cups

Cook time: 11 minutes |Serves: 4| Per serving: Calories 499; Carbs 46g; Fat 24g; Protein 25g

Ingredients:

- o   Crusty rolls – 4 (3-by-4-inch)
- o   Gouda – 4 thin slices
- o   Eggs – 5
- o   Heavy cream – 2 tbsps.
- o   Dried thyme – ½ tsp.
- o   Precooked bacon – 3 strips, chopped
- o   Salt and ground pepper to taste

Directions:

Cut the tops off the rolls and remove the insides to make a shell with about ½-inch of bread remaining. Use a slice of cheese to line the rolls, pressing down gently, so the cheese conforms to the inside of the roll. Beat the eggs and heavy cream in a bowl. Stir in the bacon, thyme, salt, and pepper. Pour the egg mixture into the rolls over the cheese. Bake at 330F until the eggs are puffy and starting to brown on top, about 8 to 12 minutes.

Mixed Berry Muffins

Cook time: 15 minutes |Serves: 8| Per serving: Calories 230; Carbs 30g; Fat 11g; Protein 4g

Ingredients:

- o   Flour – 1 1/3 cups, plus 1 tbsp.
- o   Baking powder – 2 tsps.
- o   White sugar – ¼ cup
- o   Brown sugar – 2 tbsps.

- o Eggs – 2

- o Whole milk – 2/3 cup

- o Safflower oil – 1/3 cup

- o Mixed fresh berries – 1 cup

Directions:

Combine the 1 1/3 cups flour, brown sugar, white sugar, and baking powder in a bowl and mix well. Combine the milk, eggs, and oil in another bowl and beat until mixed. Stir the egg mix into the dry ingredients. Mix until just combined. In another bowl, toss the mixed berries with the remaining 1 tbsp. flour until coated. Stir gently into the batter. Fold 16 foil muffin cups to make 8 cups. Put 4 cups into the basket and fill ¾ full with the batter. Bake at 320F until cooked, about 12 to 17 minutes. Repeat with the remaining batter and muffin cups. Cool and serve.

Dutch Pancake
Cook time: 15 minutes |Serves: 4| Per serving: Calories 196; Carbs 22g; Fat 9g; Protein 7g

Ingredients:

- o Unsalted butter – 2 tbsps.

- o Eggs – 3

- o Flour – ½ cup

- o Milk – ½ cup

- o Vanilla – ½ tsp.

- o Sliced fresh strawberries – 1 ½ cups

- o Powdered sugar – 2 tbsps.

Directions:

Preheat the air fryer with a pan in the basket at 330F. Add the butter and melt. Meanwhile, beat the eggs, milk, flour, and vanilla in a bowl until frothy. Remove from the air fryer. Pour in the batter and tilt, so the butter covers the bottom of the pan and put back in the fryer. Bake at 330F until the pancake is puffed and golden brown, about 12 to 16 minutes. Remove and top with strawberries and powdered sugar. Serve.

Spinach and Cheese Omelette
Cook time: 8 minutes |Serves: 2| Per serving: Calories 209; Carbs 1g; Fat 15.9g; Protein 15.4g

Ingredients:

- o   Eggs – 3
- o   Shredded cheese – ½ cup
- o   Chopped fresh spinach – 2 tbsps.
- o   Salt and pepper to taste

Directions:

Whisk the eggs and with salt and pepper and place in a flat dish. Add the cheese and spinach. Do not stir. Cook at 390F for 8 minutes in the air fryer. Check the consistency of the omelette. Cook for another 2 minutes if a browner omelette is desired. Enjoy.

Baked Eggs
Cook time: 20 minutes |Serves: 4| Per serving: Calories 321; Carbs 15g; Fat 6g; Protein 12g

Ingredients:

- o   Eggs – 4
- o   Baby spinach – 1 pound, torn
- o   Ham – 7 ounces, chopped
- o   Milk – 4 tbsps.
- o   Olive oil – 1 tbsp.
- o   Cooking spray
- o   Salt and black pepper to taste

Directions:

Heat oil in a pan over medium heat. Add baby spinach and stir-fry for 2 minutes and remove from heat. Use cooking spray to grease 4 ramekins and divide ham and baby spinach in each. Crack an egg in each ramekin. Also divide milk, and season with salt and pepper. Place ramekins in the preheated air fryer at 350F and bake for 20 minutes. Serve.

Breakfast Soufflé
Cook time: 8 minutes |Serves: 4| Per serving: Calories 300; Carbs 15g; Fat 7g; Protein 6g

Ingredients:

- o Eggs – 4, whisked

- o Heavy cream – 4 tbsps.

- o Red chili pepper – 1 pinch crushed

- o Parsley – 2 tbsps. chopped

- o Chives – 2 tbsps. chopped

- o Salt and black pepper to taste

Directions:

In a bowl, mix eggs with chives, parsley, red chili pepper, heavy cream, salt, and pepper. Mix well and divide into 4 soufflé dishes. Arrange dishes in the air fryer and cook at 350F for 8 minutes. Serve hot.

Cinnamon Toast

Cook time: 5 minutes |Serves: 6 | Per serving: Calories 221; Carbs 12g; Fat 4g; Protein 8g

Ingredients:

- o Butter – 1 stick, soft

- o Bread – 12 slices

- o Sugar – ½ cup

- o Vanilla extract – 1 ½ tsps.

- o Cinnamon powder – 1 ½ tsps.

Directions:

In a bowl, mix soft butter with cinnamon, vanilla, and sugar, and whisk well. Spread this on bread slices. Place them in the air fryer and cook at 400F for 5 minutes. Serve.

Turkey Burrito

Cook time: 10 minutes |Serves: 2| Per serving: Calories 349; Carbs 20g; Fat 23g; Protein 21g

Ingredients:

- o Turkey breast – 4 slices, cooked

- o Red bell pepper – 1/2, sliced

- o Eggs – 2

- ○ Small avocado – 1, peeled, pitted, and sliced

- ○ Salsa – 2 tbsps.

- ○ Salt and black pepper to taste

- ○ Mozzarella cheese – 1/8 cup, grated

- ○ Tortillas for serving

Directions:

In a bowl, whisk the eggs with salt and pepper. Pour them in a pan and place in the air fryer's basket. Cook at 400F for 5 minutes. Remove and transfer eggs to a plate. Arrange tortillas on a working surface. Divide eggs, turkey meat, bell pepper, cheese, salsa, and avocado on them. Roll the burritos. Line the air fryer basket with tin foil and place the burritos on it. Heat up the burritos at 300F for 3 minutes. Serve.

Breakfast Fish Tacos

Cook time: 13 minutes |Serves: 4| Per serving: Calories 200; Carbs 9g; Fat 3g; Protein 5g

Ingredients:

- ○ Big tortillas – 4

- ○ Red bell pepper – 1, chopped

- ○ Yellow onion – 1, chopped

- ○ Corn – 1 cup

- ○ Whitefish fillets – 4, skinless, and boneless

- ○ Salsa – ½ cup

- ○ Mixed romaine lettuce, spinach, and radicchio – 1 handful

- ○ Parmesan – 4 tbsps. grated

Directions:

Put fish fillets in the air fryer and cook at 350F for 6 minutes. Meanwhile, heat up a pan over medium-high heat; add corn, onion, and bell pepper — Stir-Fry for 2 minutes. On your work surface, arrange tortillas. And build your tacos with all the ingredients. Roll the tacos, place them in the preheated air fryer and cook at 350F for 6 minutes more. Divide fish tacos between plates and serve.

Shrimp Frittata

Cook time: 15 minutes |Serves: 4| Per serving: Calories 162; Carbs 8g; Fat 6g; Protein 4g

Ingredients:

- Eggs – 4
- Basil – ½ tsp. dried
- Cooking spray
- Salt and black pepper to taste
- Rice – ½ cup, cooked
- Shrimp – ½ cup, cooked, peeled, deveined, and chopped
- Baby spinach – ½ cup, chopped
- Monterey jack cheese – ½ cup, grated

Directions:

In a bowl, mix eggs with basil, pepper, and salt. Whisk well. Grease the air fryer's basket with cooking spray and add shrimp, spinach, and rice. Add egg mix, sprinkle cheese all over and cook in the air fryer at 350F for 10 minutes. Serve.

Tuna Sandwiches

Cook time: 5 minutes |Serves: 4| Per serving: Calories 182; Carbs 8g; Fat 4g; Protein 6g

Ingredients:

- Canned tuna – 16 ounces, drained
- Mayonnaise – ¼ cup
- Mustard – 2 tbsps.
- Lemon juice - 1 tbsp.
- Green onions – 2, chopped
- English muffins – 3, halved
- Butter – 3 tbsps.
- Provolone cheese - 6

Directions:

In a bowl, mix mayo, tuna, lemon juice, mustard, and green onions. Grease muffin halves with butter. Place them in the preheated air fryer and bake them at 350F for 4 minutes. Add tuna mix on muffin halves, then top each with cheese. Return sandwiches to air fryer and bake 4 minutes more. Serve.

Tuna and Zucchini Tortillas

Cook time: 10 minutes |Serves: 4| Per serving: Calories 162; Carbs 9g; Fat 4g; Protein 4g

Ingredients:

- o   Corn tortillas – 4
- o   Butter – 4 tbsps. soft
- o   Canned tuna – 6 ounces, drained
- o   Zucchini – 1 cup, shredded
- o   Mayonnaise – 1/3 cup
- o   Mustard – 2 tbsps.
- o   Cheddar cheese – 1 cup, grated

Directions:

Spread butter on tortillas. Put them in the air fryer basket and cook them at 400F for 3 minutes. Meanwhile, in a bowl, mix tuna with mustard, mayo, and zucchini and stir. Split this mixture on each tortilla, top with cheese and roll tortillas. Cook at 400F for 4 minutes more. Serve.

Shrimp Croquettes

Cook time: 8 minutes |Serves: 4| Per serving: Calories 142; Carbs 9g; Fat 4g; Protein 4g

Ingredients:

- o   Shrimp – 2/3 pound, cooked, peeled, deveined and chopped
- o   Bread crumbs – 1 ½ cups
- o   Egg – 1, whisked
- o   Lemon juice – 2 tbsps.
- o   Green onions – 3, chopped
- o   Basil – ½ tsp. dried

- o   Salt and black pepper to taste

- o   Olive oil – 2 tbsps.

Directions:

Mix half of the bread crumbs with lemon juice, and egg in a bowl and stir well. Add shrimp, salt, pepper, basil, and green onions. Stir well. In another bowl, mix the rest of the bread crumbs with the oil and toss well. Shape round balls out of the shrimp mix, dredge them in bread crumbs. Place them in the preheated air fryer and cook for 8 minutes, at 400F. Serve.

Shrimp Pancake

Cook time: 10 minutes |Serves: 2| Per serving: Calories 200; Carbs 12g; Fat 6g; Protein 4g

Ingredients:

- o   Butter – 1 tbsp.

- o   Eggs – 3, whisked

- o   Flour – ½ cup

- o   Milk – ½ cup

- o   Salsa – 1 cup

- o   Small shrimp – 1 cup, peeled and deveined

Directions:

Preheat the air fryer at 400F. Add fryer pan, add 1 tbsp. butter and melt it. Mix eggs with milk and flour in a bowl. Whisk well and pour into the air fryer pan, spread. Cook at 350F for 12 minutes and transfer to a plate. Mix shrimp and salsa in a bowl. Stir and serve pancake with this on the side.

Chicken Sandwiches

Cook time: 10 minutes |Serves: 4| Per serving: Calories 126; Carbs 14g; Fat 4g; Protein 4g

Ingredients:

- o   Chicken breasts – 2, skinless, boneless, and cubed

- o   Red onion – 1, chopped

- o   Red bell pepper – 1, sliced

- o   Italian seasoning – ½ cup

- ○ Thyme – ½ tsp. dried

- ○ Butter lettuce – 2 cups, torn

- ○ Pita pockets – 4

- ○ Cherry tomatoes – 1 cup, halved

- ○ Olive oil – 1 tbsp.

Directions:

In the air fryer, mix chicken with oil, Italian seasoning, bell pepper, onion, toss and cook at 380F for 10 minutes. Transfer chicken mixture to a bowl, add cherry tomatoes, butter lettuce, and thyme. Toss well. Stuff pita pockets with this mixture and serve.

Chapter 2 Vegetarian and Vegan

Mediterranean Vegetables

Cook time: 20 minutes |Serves: 4| Per serving: Calories 281; Carbs 21g; Fat 21g; Protein 2g

Ingredients:

- Cherry tomatoes – 1.76 oz.
- Large courgetti – 1
- Green pepper – 1
- Large parsnip – 1
- Carrot – 1
- Mixed herbs – 1 tsp.
- Honey – 2 tbsps.
- Mustard – 1 tsp.
- Garlic puree – 2 tsps.
- Olive oil – 6 tbsps.
- Salt and pepper to taste

Directions:

Chop the vegetables. Add courgetti, green pepper, tomatoes, parsnip, and carrot to the air fryer basket. Drizzle with 3 tbsps. oil and cook for 15 minutes at 350F. Meantime, mix up the rest of the ingredients and place them in the air fryer basket. Shake well so all the vegetables are cover with the mixture. Cook for 5 minutes at 390F. Serve.

Air Fryer Carrots

Cook time: 20 minutes |Serves: 4| Per serving: Calories 126; Carbs 17g; Fat 6g; Protein 1g

Ingredients:

- o Carrots – 1 lb. peeled
- o Olive oil – 2 tbsps.
- o Grated parmesan cheese – ¼ cup
- o Salt and pepper to taste
- o Garlic powder – ½ tsp.
- o Paprika – ½ tsp.
- o Fresh chopped parsley to taste

Directions:

In a bowl, place the carrots and toss them with oil, garlic powder, and paprika. Cook in the air fryer at 380F for 20 minutes. Shake the basket at the halfway mark. Top with parmesan cheese and parsley. Season with salt and pepper and serve.

Air Fried Quinoa

Cook time: 21 minutes |Serves: 4| Per serving: Calories 159; Carbs 27g; Fat 3g; Protein 6g

Ingredients:

- o Quinoa – 2 cups, rinsed
- o Water – 2 cups

Directions:

Place the rinsed quinoa in the air fryer basket and cook for 2 minutes at 320F. Then add water, mix and cook for 5 minutes at 320F. Serve.

Crispy Chickpeas

Cook time: 20 minutes |Serves: 2| Per serving: Calories 263; Carbs 48.1g; Fat 4.8g; Protein 10.5g

Ingredients:

- o Chickpeas – 1(15 oz.) can, drained and rinsed
- o Olive oil – 1 tsp.

○ Dry ranch seasoning mix – 1 tbsp.

Directions:

Mix oil and chickpeas in a bowl. Spread the mixture in the air fryer basket and cook at 390F for 17 minutes. Shake once at the halfway mark. Remove and toss with seasoning. Serve.

Fried Cauliflower

Cook time: 15 minutes |Serves: 4| Per serving: Calories 457; Carbs 67g; Fat 9.9g; Protein 24.3g

Ingredients:

○ Chickpeas – 15 oz.

○ Olive oil – 1 tsp.

○ Cauliflower – 1 lb. cut into florets

○ Salt – ½ tsp.

○ Ground pepper – ¼ tsp.

○ Lemon slices for garnish

Sauce mixture

○ Olive oil – ¼ cup
○ Grated Parmesan cheese – ¼ cup
○ Finely chopped parsley – 1 tbsp.
○ Lemon juice – 1 tbsp.
○ Lemon zest – 1 tsp.
○ Salt and ground pepper to taste

Directions:

In a bowl, combine the cauliflower, oil, salt, and pepper. Mix. Cook in the air fryer for 15 minutes at 400F. Stir. Meanwhile, mix the sauce ingredients in a bowl. Serve.

Brussels Sprouts

Cook time: 10 minutes |Serves: 2| Per serving: Calories 72; Carbs 1.6g; Fat 7.1g; Protein 0.5g

Ingredients:

○ Brussels sprouts – 2 cups, chopped

○ Olive oil – 1 tbsp.

- o   Balsamic vinegar -1 tbsp.
- o   Salt – ¼ tsp.

Directions:

Mix everything in a bowl. Bake in the air fryer at 400F for 10 minutes. Shake at 5 minutes and then at 8 minutes mark. Serve.

Veggie Cake
Cook time: 12 minutes |Serves: 2| Per serving: Calories 37; Carbs 2g; Fat 3g; Protein 0.4g

Ingredients:

- o   Leftover vegetable bake – 1 cup
- o   Plain flour – 1 tbsp.

Directions:

Preheat the air fryer at 350F. Mix the flour and veggies. Make a thick dough. Grease the basket with cooking spray. Cook at 350F for 12 minutes. Flip at the halfway mark. Slice and serve.

Stuffed Garlic Mushrooms
Cook time: 25 minutes |Serves: 4| Per serving: Calories 43; Carbs 3g; Fat 3g; Protein 1g

Ingredients:

- o   Small mushrooms – 8
- o   Chopped onion – 0.7 oz.
- o   Breadcrumbs – 1 tbsp.
- o   Garlic puree – 1 tsp.
- o   Oil – 1 tbsp.
- o   Parsley – 1 tsp.
- o   Salt and pepper to taste

Directions:

In a bowl, mix everything except for the mushrooms. Remove the middle stalks from the mushrooms and fill the middle area with the breadcrumb mixture. Bake in the air fryer at 350F for 10 minutes. Serve.

Air-Fried Brussels Sprouts

Cook time: 16 minutes |Serves: 2| Per serving: Calories 202; Carbs 15.9g; Fat 12.32g; Protein 6.89g

Ingredients:

- o Grated parmesan – 2 tbsps.

- o Brussels sprouts – ½ lb. sliced

- o Garlic powder – 1 tsp.

- o Oil – 1 tbsp.

- o Caesar dressing for dipping

- o Salt and pepper to taste

Directions:

Mix everything except for the parmesan in a bowl. Coat well and cook in the air fryer at 350F for 8 minutes. Then toss and cook 8 minutes more. Garnish with parmesan and serve.

Green Beans

Cook time: 14 minutes |Serves: 4| Per serving: Calories 82; Carbs 6.3g; Fat 5.66g; Protein 1.5g

Ingredients:

- o Olive oil – 1 tbsp.

- o Fresh green beans – 1 lb. with ends trimmed and cut into halves

- o Garlic powder – ½ tsp.

- o Salt and pepper to taste

- o Fresh lemon slices

Directions:

Combine green beans with garlic powder in a bowl and season with salt and pepper. Bake in the air fryer at 360F for 10 to 14 minutes. Shake twice during cooking. Garnish with lemon slices and serve.

Roasted Asparagus

Cook time: 10 minutes |Serves: 4| Per serving: Calories 52; Carbs 5.72g; Fat 1.97g; Protein 2.95g

Ingredients:

- o   Asparagus – 1 lb. ends trimmed

- o   Olive oil – 2 tsps.

- o   Salt and black pepper to taste

Directions:

Coat the asparagus with oil and season with salt and pepper. Cook in the air fryer at 380F for 7 to 10 minutes. Shake once. Serve.

Crispy Broccoli

Cook time: 10 minutes |Serves: 4| Per serving: Calories 104; Carbs 5.42g; Fat 7.41g; Protein 3.39g

Ingredients:

- o   Cooking oil – 2 tbsps.

- o   Broccoli – 1 lb. chopped

- o   Garlic powder – ½ tsp.

- o   Salt and pepper to taste

- o   Fresh lemon wedges

Directions:

Add broccoli to a bowl and drizzle with oil. Season with salt, pepper, and garlic powder. Mix and cook in the air fryer at 380F for 12 to 15 minutes. Shake the basket 3 times during cooking. Serve with lemon wedges.

Acorn Squash

Cook time: 20 minutes |Serves: 4| Per serving: Calories 152; Carbs 27.74g; Fat 7.73g; Protein 2.63g

Ingredients:

- o   Acorn squash – 1, cut into half an inch thick cubes

- o   Butter – 3 tbsps. melted

- o   Brown sugar – 2 tsps.

- o   Kosher salt and black pepper to taste

- o   Chopped nuts and melted butter for topping

Directions:

In a bowl, combine melted butter, brown sugar, season with salt and pepper. Add in the acorn squash and mix. Cook in the air fryer at 375F for 15 to 20 minutes. Flip after 10 minutes of cooking. Serve with toppings.

Air-Fried Avocado
Cook time: 6 minutes |Serves: 2| Per serving: Calories 274; Carbs 23g; Fat 18g; Protein 5g

Ingredients:

- o   All-purpose flour – ½ cup
- o   Avocados – 2, cut into wedges
- o   Eggs – 2
- o   Mayonnaise – 2 tbsps.
- o   Apple cider vinegar – 1 tbsp.
- o   Sriracha chili sauce – 1 tbsp.
- o   Black pepper – ½ tsps.
- o   Kosher salt – ¼ tsp.
- o   Panko breadcrumbs – ½ cup
- o   No-salt-added ketchup – ¼ cup
- o   Water – 1 tbsp.
- o   Cooking spray

Directions:

Arrange three bowls. Add flour, and pepper in the first bowl, beaten eggs in the second bowl, and breadcrumbs in a third bowl. Dredge avocado wedges in the flour, then egg and dip in the breadcrumbs. Coat well and spray with cooking oil. Bake in the air fryer at 400F for 4 minutes. Then flip the avocados and cook for 2 minutes more. Remove and season with salt. Mix the remaining ingredients to make a sauce. Serve.

Rosemary Potatoes
Cook time: 15 minutes |Serves: 2| Per serving: Calories 201; Carbs 22.71g; Fat 10.71g; Protein 3.34g

Ingredients:

- o   Vegetable oil – 3 tbsps.

- o   Yellow baby potatoes – 4, quartered

- o   Dried rosemary minced – 2 tsps.

- o   Minced garlic – 1 tbsp.

- o   Ground black pepper – 1 tsp.

- o   Chopped parsley – ¼ cup

- o   Fresh lime juice – 1 tbsp.

- o   Salt -1 tsp.

Directions:

In a bowl, add potatoes, garlic, rosemary, pepper, and salt. Mix well. Bake in the air fryer at 400F for 15 minutes. Flip the potatoes at the halfway mark. Then sprinkle with lemon juice and parsley and serve.

Falafel Balls

Cook time: 12 minutes |Serves: 3| Per serving: Calories 762; Carbs 74g; Fat 38g; Protein 22g

Ingredients:

- o   Sweet onion – ½ cup, diced

- o   Oil – 2 tbsps.

- o   Turmeric – ½ tsp.

- o   Carrots – ½ cup, minced

- o   Rolled oats -1 cup

- o   Roasted, salted cashews – ½ cup

- o   Cooked chickpeas – 2 cups, drained and rinsed

- o   Juice of 1 lemon

- o   Soy sauce – 2 tbsps.

- o   Flax meal – 1 tbsp.

- o   Garlic powder – ½ tsp.

o   Ground cumin – ½

Directions:

Heat a little oil and sauté onions and carrots in the Instant Pot Duo. Cook for 7 minutes, then transfer to a bowl. Place cashew and oats in a food processor and process until you get a coarse meal consistency. Add this mixture to the bowl with vegetables. Place the chickpeas, lemon juice and soy sauce into the food processor and puree until a semi-smooth consistency. Transfer it to the bowl and add in the flax and spices. Mix well. Form falafel balls. Line the air fryer with parchment paper. Cook the balls in the air fryer at 370F for 12 minutes. Shake the basket after 8 minutes of cooking. Serve.

Brussels Sprout Chips
Cook time: 8 minutes |Serves: 3| Per serving: Calories 210; Carbs 12g; Fat 16.4g; Protein 6g

Ingredients:

o   Brussels sprouts – ½ pound, sliced

o   Garlic powder - 1 tsp.

o   Olive oil – 1 tbsp.

o   Parmesan – 2 tbsps. plus 2 tbsps. shredded

o   Ground black pepper and salt to taste

o   Caesar dressing – ¼ cup for dipping

Directions:

Toss 2 tbsps. Parmesan, sliced Brussels, and garlic powder in a bowl. Season with salt and pepper. Bake in the air fryer at 350F for 8 minutes. Shake at the halfway mark. Then remove and garnish with parmesan. Serve with Caesar dressing.

Crispy Potatoes
Cook time: 18 minutes |Serves: 4| Per serving: Calories 133; Carbs 24g; Fat 3.6g; Protein 3g

Ingredients:

o   Baby potatoes – 1 pound, chopped with peel

o   Oil – 1 tbsp.

o   Italian seasoning – 1 tsp.

- o   Garlic powder – 1 tsp.

- o   Cajun seasoning – 1 tsp.

- o   Salt and pepper to taste

- o   Lemons – 2, cut into wedges

- o   Chopped parsley – ¼ cup, for garnish

Directions:

Toss garlic powder, halved potatoes, Cajun seasoning, Italian seasoning, salt in a bowl and mix with potatoes. Bake in the air fryer at 400F for 18 minutes. Shake the potatoes after 10 minutes of cooking. Finish cooking and serve with lemon wedges and parsley.

Honey-Glazed Carrots

Cook time: 35 minutes |Serves: 6 | Per serving: Calories 146; Carbs 19g; Fat 8g; Protein 1g

Ingredients:

- o   Carrots – 2 pounds, peeled and cut lengthwise

- o   Honey – 2 tbsps.

- o   Butter – ¼ cup

- o   Garlic powder – ½ tsp.

- o   Rosemary – ½ tsp. dried

- o   Salt and pepper to taste

- o   Fresh thyme – 4 tbsps. chopped

Directions:

Melt butter in a saucepan. Add garlic powder, rosemary, honey, pepper, and salt and mix well. Remove and set aside. Add the carrots and mix. Preheat the air fryer at 400F. Line the air fryer basket with a baking sheet and cook the carrots at 400F for 35 minutes. Garnish and serve.

Bang Bang Cauliflower

Cook time: 12 minutes |Serves: 4| Per serving: Calories 100; Carbs 12g; Fat 5g; Protein 4g

Ingredients:

- o   Cauliflower – 21 ounces, chopped

- o   Olive oil – 3 tbsps.

- o   Garlic – 3 cloves, grated

- o   Lime zest of 1 lime

- o   Sriracha – 1 tbsp.

- o   Sweet chili sauce - 2 tbsps.

- o   Salt and pepper to taste

- o   Chopped cilantro – 1 tsp. for garnish

Directions:

Combine oil, chili sauce, lime juice, sriracha, and garlic in a bowl. Add the cauliflower, ground pepper, salt and mix. Cook in the air fryer at 360F for 12 minutes. Shake the basket at the halfway mark. Garnish and serve.

Roasted Carrots

Cook time: 30 minutes |Serves: 4 | Per serving: Calories 137; Carbs 23g; Fat 5.1g; Protein 2g

Ingredients:

- o   Carrots – 2 pounds, quartered

- o   Olive oil – 3 tbsps.

- o   Black pepper and salt to taste

- o   Chopped parsley – ¼ cup, fresh for garnish

Directions:

Combine everything in a bowl, except for the parsley. Mix well. Cook in the air fryer at 400F for 30 minutes. Shake the basket at the halfway mark. Serve with chopped parsley.

Garlic Rosemary Brussels Sprouts

Cook time: 13 minutes |Serves: 4| Per serving: Calories 154; Carbs 13g; Fat 10.6g; Protein 4g

Ingredients:

- o   Brussels sprouts – 1 pound, halved

- o   Olive oil - 3 tbsps.

- o   Panko breadcrumbs – ½ cup

- o   Garlic – 2 cloves, chopped

- o   Salt and pepper to taste

- o   Chopped fresh rosemary -1 ½ tsps.

Directions:

In a bowl, put pepper, salt, garlic, and oil and microwave for 30 seconds. Preheat the air fryer for 5 minutes at 350F. Mix the Brussels sprouts in the heated oil mixture. Cook in the air fryer for 8 minutes. Shake the basket after 5 minutes and then finish cooking. In a bowl combine breadcrumbs, remaining oil mixture and rosemary. When the cooking is over, open the air fryer and sprinkle the breadcrumb mixture over the sprouts. Close and cook for 5 minutes more. Serve.

Air Fryer Chickpeas
Cook time: 20 minutes |Serves:4 | Per serving: Calories 154; Carbs 25g; Fat 3.1g; Protein 8g

Ingredients:

- o   Canned chickpeas – 15 ½ ounces, rinsed and drained

- o   Cumin powder – ¼ tsp.

- o   Cayenne pepper powder – ¼ tsp.

- o   Salt – 1 tsp.

- o   Cooking spray

Directions:

Cook the chickpeas in the air fryer at 390F for 20 minutes. Meantime, combine cumin powder, cayenne pepper, and salt in a bowl. After 5 minutes, open the lid and spray some oil on the chickpeas. Sprinkle a quarter of the seasoning and stir the chickpeas with a spoon. Close and continue to cook. Shake the basket after every 5 minutes. Remove from the air fryer and add the remaining seasoning. Mix and serve.

Bang Bang Broccoli
Cook time: 20 minutes |Serves: 4| Per serving: Calories 109; Carbs 10g; Fat 5.7g; Protein 8g

Ingredients:

- o   Broccoli – 2 pounds, chopped

- o   Extra-virgin olive oil – 3 tbsps.

- o Sriracha – 1 tbsp.

- o Sweet chili sauce – 2 tbsps.

- o Lime zest – 1

- o Salt and pepper to taste

Directions:

Preheat the air fryer at 425F for 5 minutes. Whisk sriracha, chili sauce, lime zest, and oil in a bowl. Mix the broccoli with the sauce. Add salt and pepper and mix again. Cook in the air fryer for 20 minutes. Shake once. Serve.

Tofu Italian Style
Cook time: 10 minutes |Serves: 2| Per serving: Calories 342; Carbs 16g; Fat 24.4g; Protein 21g

Ingredients:

- o Tofu – 8 ounces, extra-firm, drained, sliced lengthwise and excess water removed

- o Broth – 1 tbsp.

- o Soy sauce – 1 tbsp.

- o Basil – ½ tsp. dried

- o Oregano – ½ tsp. dried

- o Onion powder – ½ tsp.

- o Garlic powder – ½ tsp.

- o Black pepper and salt to taste

Directions:

Slice the tofu into cubes and put in a Ziplock bag. Mix all the ingredients in a bowl. Add this mixture to the Ziplock bag and mix well. Preheat the air fryer at 400F for 5 minutes. Add the seasoned tofu in the air fryer and cook at 350F for 6 minutes. Open the air fryer after 4 minutes and shake the basket. Finish cooking. Serve.

Sweet Potato Tots
Cook time: 14 minutes |Serves: 4| Per serving: Calories 78; Carbs 19g; Fat 0g; Protein 1g

Ingredients:

- o Sweet potatoes – 14 ounces, peeled and washed

- o Potato starch – 1 tbsp.

- o Garlic powder – 1/8 tsp.

- o Salt to taste

- o Saltless ketchup – ¾ cup

- o Oil for cooking

Directions:

Boil the sweet potatoes for 15 minutes until they become tender. Then cool, and shred the sweet potatoes. Add salt, garlic powder, and potato starch. Make 24 tots from this mixture. Grease the air fryer basket with oil. Place the tots in the basket and spray with cooking spray. Cook at 400F for 14 minutes. Shake the basket at the halfway mark. Serve with ketchup.

Creamy Endives

Cook time: 10 minutes |Serves: 6| Per serving: Calories 100; Carbs 7g; Fat 2g; Protein 4

Ingredients:

- o Endives – 6, trimmed and halved

- o Garlic powder – 1 tsp.

- o Greek yogurt – ½ cup

- o Curry powder – ½ tsp.

- o Salt and black pepper to taste

- o Lemon juice – 3 tbsps.

Directions:

In a bowl, mix endives with lemon juice, salt, pepper, curry powder, yogurt, and garlic powder. Coat well and set aside for 10 minutes. Cook in the preheated 350F air fryer for 10 minutes. Serve.

Zucchini Fries

Cook time: 12 minutes |Serves: 4 | Per serving: Calories 172; Carbs 7g; Fat 3g; Protein 3g

Ingredients:

- o Zucchini – 1, cut into medium sticks

- o   Olive oil – 1 drizzle

- o   Salt and black pepper to taste

- o   Eggs – 2, whisked

- o   Bread crumbs – 1 cup

- o   Flour – ½ cup

Directions:

In a bowl, add flour and mix with salt and pepper. Put breadcrumbs in another bowl. In a third bowl, mix the egg with salt and pepper. Dredge zucchini fries in flour, then in eggs and in bread crumbs. Grease the air fryer with olive oil. Heat up at 400F. Add zucchini fries and cook them for 12 minutes. Serve.

Balsamic Artichokes

Cook time: 7 minutes |Serves: 4| Per serving: Calories 200; Carbs 12g; Fat 3g; Protein 4g

Ingredients:

- o   Big artichokes – 4, trimmed

- o   Salt and black pepper to taste

- o   Lemon juice – 2 tbsps.

- o   Extra-virgin olive oil – ¼ cup

- o   Balsamic vinegar – 2 tsps.

- o   Oregano – 1 tsp. dried

- o   Garlic – 2 cloves, minced

Directions:

Season artichokes with salt and pepper. Rub with half of the lemon juice and half of the oil. Cook in the air fryer at 360F for 7 minutes. Meanwhile, in a bowl, mix the remaining oil, and lemon juice with vinegar, salt, pepper, garlic, and oregano. Mix well. Arrange artichokes on a platter. Drizzle the balsamic vinaigrette over them and serve.

Beet Salad and Parsley Dressing

Cook time: 14 minutes |Serves: 4| Per serving: Calories 70; Carbs 6g; Fat 2g; Protein 4g

Ingredients:

- o   Beets – 4

- o   Balsamic vinegar – 2 tbsps.

- o   Parsley – 1 bunch, chopped

- o   Salt and black pepper to taste

- o   Extra-virgin olive oil – 1 tbsp.

- o   Garlic – 1 clove, chopped

- o   Capers – 2 tbsps.

Directions:

Put beets in the air fryer and cook at 360F for 14 minutes. Meanwhile, in a bowl, mix garlic, parsley, olive oil, salt, pepper, and capers and mix well. Remove the beets, and cool. Peel and slice them. Add vinegar, drizzle the parsley dressing over and serve.

Broccoli Salad
Cook time: 8 minutes |Serves: 4| Per serving: Calories 121; Carbs 4g; Fat 3g; Protein 4g

Ingredients:

- o   Broccoli – 1 head, florets separated

- o   Peanut oil – 1 tbsp.

- o   Garlic – 6 cloves, minced

- o   Chinese rice wine vinegar – 1 tbsp.

- o   Salt and black pepper to taste

Directions:

In a bowl, mix broccoli with half of the oil, salt, and pepper and toss. Cook in the air fryer at 350F for 8 minutes. Shake once. Transfer broccoli to a bowl. Add the rest of the peanut oil, rice vinegar, and garlic, and toss well. Serve.

Brussels Sprouts and Tomatoes Mix
Cook time: 10 minutes |Serves: 4| Per serving: Calories 121; Carbs 11g; Fat 4g; Protein 4g

Ingredients:

- o   Brussels sprouts – 1 pound, trimmed

- o   Salt and black pepper to taste

- o   Cherry tomatoes – 8, halved

- o   Green onions – ¼ cup, chopped

- o   Olive oil – 1 tbsp.

Directions:

Season Brussels sprouts with salt and pepper. Cook in the air fryer at 350F for 10 minutes. Transfer to a bowl. Add olive oil, green onions, cherry tomatoes, salt, and pepper. Toss and serve.

Spicy Cabbage
Cook time: 8 minutes |Serves: 4| Per serving: Calories 100; Carbs 11g; Fat 4g; Protein 7g

Ingredients:

- o   Cabbage – 1, cut into 8 wedges

- o   Sesame seed oil – 1 tbsp.

- o   Carrot – 1, grated

- o   Apple cider vinegar – ¼ cup

- o   Apple juice – ¼ cup

- o   Cayenne pepper – ½ tsp.

- o   Red pepper flakes – 1 tsp. crushed

Directions:

In a pan, combine cabbage with pepper flakes, cayenne, apple juice, vinegar, carrot, and oil. Toss to mix. Place the pan in the preheated air fryer and cook at 350F for 8 minutes. Divide cabbage mix between plates and serve.

Collard Greens Mix
Cook time: 10 minutes |Serves: 4| Per serving: Calories 121; Carbs 7g; Fat 3g; Protein 3g

Ingredients:

- o   Collard greens – 1 bunch, trimmed

- o   Olive oil – 2 tbsps.

- o   Tomato paste – 2 tbsps.

- o Yellow onion – 1, chopped

- o Garlic – 3 cloves, minced

- o Salt and black pepper to taste

- o Balsamic vinegar – 1 tbsp.

- o Sugar – 1 tsp.

Directions:

In a bowl, mix tomato puree, onion, vinegar, garlic, and oil. Whisk. Add sugar, salt, pepper, and collard greens. Mix. Place the bowl in the air fryer and cook at 320F for 10 minutes. Serve.

Eggplant and Zucchini Mix

Cook time: 8 minutes |Serves: 4| Per serving: Calories 152; Carbs 19g; Fat 5g; Protein 5g

Ingredients:

- o Eggplant – 1, cubed

- o Zucchinis – 3, roughly cubed

- o Lemon juice - 2 tbsps.

- o Salt and black pepper to taste

- o Thyme – 1 tsp. dried

- o Oregano – 1 tsp. dried

- o Olive oil – 3 tbsps.

Directions:

Put eggplant in a dish. Add olive oil, oregano, thyme, salt, pepper, lemon juice, and zucchinis. Toss to mix. Place the dish in the air fryer and at 360F for 8 minutes. Serve.

Chapter 3 Poultry

Spiced Chicken Legs

Cook time: 50 minutes |Serves: 6 | Per serving: Calories 222; Carbs 1g; Fat 14g; Protein 23g

Ingredients:

- o Chicken drumsticks – 2.5 lbs.
- o Olive oil – 2 tbsps.
- o Salt and pepper to taste
- o Garlic powder – 1 tsp.
- o Smoked paprika – 1 tsp.
- o Cumin – ½ tsp.

Directions:

In a bowl, add drumsticks with oil and mix. In another bowl, mix the other ingredients then coat the drumsticks with the mixture. Cook the chicken at 400F for 25 minutes in batches. Shake the basket at the halfway mark. Chicken is cooked when it reaches 165F. Serve.

Herbed Turkey Breast

Cook time: 1 hour |Serves: 8| Per serving: Calories 215; Carbs 8.3g; Fat 6.7g; Protein 29.4g

Ingredients:

- o Turkey breast – 3 lbs.

Rub ingredients

- o Olive oil – 2 tbsps.

- o Lemon juice – 2 tbsps.

- o Minced garlic – 1 tbsp.

- o Ground mustard – 2 tsps.

- o Salt and pepper to taste

- o Dried rosemary – 1 tsp.

- o Dried thyme – 1 tsp.

- o Ground sage – 1 tsp.

Directions:

Combine the rub ingredients in a bowl and rub the turkey with it. Rub under any loose skin. Place the turkey on a cooking tray, skin side up. Cook in the air fryer at 360F for 1 hour. The turkey is done when it reaches 160F. Rest, slice and serve.

Chicken Casserole
Cook time: 15 minutes |Serves: 4| Per serving: Calories 301; Carbs 17g; Fat 17g; Protein 20g

Ingredients:

- o Chicken - 3 cups, shredded

- o Egg noodles – 1(12 oz.) bag (boiled in hot water for 2 to 3 minutes then drain)

- o Onion – ½, chopped

- o Chopped carrots – ½ cup

- o Frozen peas – ¼ cup

- o Frozen broccoli pieces – ¼ cup

- o Celery -2 stalks, chopped

- o Chicken broth – 5 cups

- o Garlic powder – 1 tsp.

- o Salt and pepper to taste

- o Cheddar cheese – 1 cup, shredded

- o French onions – 1 package

- Sour cream – ¼ cup

- Cream of chicken and mushroom soup – 1 can

Directions:

Place the chicken, vegetables, garlic powder, salt, and pepper and broth in a bowl and mix. Then place in the air fryer basket. Lightly stir the egg noodles into the mix until damp. Cook for 4 minutes at 350F. Then stir in the can of soup, sour cream, cheese and 1/3 of the French onions. Top with the remaining French onion and close. Cook for 10 minutes more. Serve.

Fried Whole Chicken
Cook time: 70 minutes |Serves: 4| Per serving: Calories 436; Carbs 4g; Fat 28g; Protein 42g

Ingredients:

- Whole chicken - 1

- Oil – 2 tbsps.

- Garlic powder – 1 tsp.

- Onion powder – 1 tsp.

- Paprika – 1 tsp.

- Italian seasoning - 1 tsp.

- Steak seasoning – 2 tbsps.

- Chicken broth – 1 ½ cups

Directions:

Mix the seasoning and rub a little amount on the chicken. Pour the broth inside the air fryer basket and place the chicken. Cook for 25 minutes at 400F. Then rub the top of the chicken with oil and rub it with half of the seasoning. Cook 10 minutes more. Then flip the chicken and grease it with oil. Rub with the remaining seasoning. Cook for 10 minutes more. Rest, slice and serve.

Turkey Breasts
Cook time: 50 minutes |Serves: 4| Per serving: Calories 558; Carbs 1g; Fat 18g; Protein 98g

Ingredients:

- Boneless turkey breast – 3 lbs.

- Mayonnaise – ¼ cup

- o Poultry seasoning – 2 tsps.

- o Salt and pepper to taste

- o Garlic powder – ½ tsp.

Directions:

Preheat the air fryer to 360F. Season the turkey with mayonnaise, seasoning, salt, garlic powder, and black pepper. Cook the turkey in the air fryer for 1 hour at 360F. Turning after every 15 minutes. The turkey is done when it reaches 165F.

BBQ Chicken Breasts
Cook time: 15 minutes |Serves: 4| Per serving: Calories 131; Carbs 2g; Fat 3g; Protein 24g

Ingredients:

- o Boneless, skinless chicken breast – 4, about 6 oz. each

- o BBQ seasoning – 2 tbsps.

- o Cooking spray

Directions:

Rub the chicken with BBQ seasoning and marinate in the refrigerator for 45 minutes. Preheat the air fryer at 400F. Grease the basket with oil and place the chicken. Then spray oil on top. Cook for 13 to 14 minutes. Flipping at the halfway mark. Serve.

Turkey Burgers
Cook time: 25 minutes |Serves: 4| Per serving: Calories 183; Carbs 11g; Fat 3g; Protein 28g

Ingredients:

- o Lean ground turkey – 1 lb.

- o Unsweetened apple sauce – ¼ cup

- o Chopped onion – ½

- o Ranch seasoning – 1 tbsp.

- o Worcestershire sauce -2 tsps.

- o Minced garlic - 1 tsp.

- o Plain breadcrumbs – ¼ cup

- o Salt and pepper to taste

Directions:

Mix everything and make 4 patties. Keep in the refrigerator for 30 minutes. Preheat the air fryer at 360F. Grease the air fryer basket with cooking spray and place in the patties. Then spray cooking spray on top. Cook for 15 minutes. Flip at the halfway mark. Serve.

Turkey Legs

Cook time: 40 minutes |Serves: 2| Per serving: Calories 458; Carbs 3g; Fat 46g; Protein 82g

Ingredients:

- o Turkey legs – 2 large, washed and pat dried
- o Smoked paprika – 1 ½ tsp.
- o Brown sugar – 1 tsp.
- o Seasoning salt – 1 tsp.
- o Garlic powder – ½ tsp.
- o Oil for spraying

Directions:

Mix the paprika, sugar, salt, and garlic powder well. Rub the turkey with seasoning mixture, rub under the skin as well. Preheat the air fryer. Spray the air fryer basket with cooking spray and place the turkey legs. Then spray the turkey with oil. Cook for 400F for 20 minutes. Then flip and spray with oil. Cook 20 minutes more. Serve.

Rotisserie Chicken

Cook time: 60 minutes |Serves: 4| Per serving: Calories 534; Carbs 0g; Fat 36g; Protein 35g

Ingredients:

- o Whole chicken – 1, cleaned and patted dry
- o Olive oil – 2 tbsps.
- o Seasoned salt – 1 tbsp.

Directions:

Remove the giblet packet from the cavity. Rub the chicken with oil and salt. Place in the air fryer basket, breast-side down. Cook at 350F for 30 minutes. Then flip and cook another 30 minutes. Chicken is done when it reaches 165F.

Greek Chicken & Potatoes

Cook time: 20 minutes |Serves: 6| Per serving: Calories 679; Carbs 22g; Fat 44.4g; Protein 47.8g

Ingredients:

- o   Chicken thighs – 12, bone-in

- o   Yellow potatoes – 1 ½ lbs. chopped

- o   Chicken broth – ½ cup

- o   Olive oil – 1/3 cup

- o   Lemon juice – 1/3 cup

- o   Lemon zest – 1 tsp.

- o   Garlic - 1 tbsp. minced

- o   Dried oregano – 2 tsps.

- o   Dried parsley – 1 tsp.

- o   Black pepper – 1 tsp.

- o   Salt – 2 tsps.

- o   Lemon wedges for garnish

Directions:

Whisk the oil, lemon juice, garlic, parsley, oregano, pepper, lemon zest, and salt in a bowl. Add the chicken broth into the Instant Pot and arrange the chicken thighs in a single layer. Pour half of the lemon juice mixture over the chicken thighs. Layer the potatoes on top of the thighs and pour the remaining half of the lemon juice mixture over the potatoes. Cook on High for 15 minutes. Open and remove the potatoes to a dish. Transfer the chicken to a platter and the juices to a bowl. Arrange the chicken in the air fryer basket to brown it. Cook at 500F for 4 minutes. Serve chicken and potato with some of the reserved juices and garnish with lemon wedges.

Chicken Fillet

Cook time: 30 minutes |Serves: 3| Per serving: Calories 265; Carbs 2g; Fat 13g; Protein 35g

Ingredients:

- o   Chicken breast fillets – 3

- o   Chicken stock – ¾ cup, divided

- o Oil – 2 tbsps. divided

- o Italian seasoning – 1 tsp.

- o Ground coriander – ½ tsp.

- o Paprika – ½ tsp.

- o Garlic – ½ tsp. minced

- o Ground ginger – ½ tsp.

- o Salt and pepper to taste

Directions:

Mix the seasoning, coriander, paprika, garlic, ginger, pepper, salt, 2 tbsps. stock, and 1 tbsp olive oil in a bowl. Coat the chicken with this mixture. Press Sauté and add oil. Cook the chicken breasts 2 minutes per side. Remove the chicken and set aside. Then add the remaining chicken stock to the Instant Pot. Place the trivet and arrange the chicken on top. Cook on High for 5 minutes. When finished, remove the chicken, and stock from the pot. Cook the chicken on the air fryer setting for 20 minutes at 350F. Flip at the halfway mark. Serve.

Honey-Mustard Chicken Breasts
Cook time: 20 minutes |Serves: 6| Per serving: Calories 236; Carbs 9.8g; Fat 5g; Protein 38g

Ingredients:

- o Boneless, skinless chicken breasts – 6 (6-oz, each)

- o Fresh rosemary – 2 tbsps. minced

- o Honey – 3 tbsps.

- o Dijon mustard – 1 tbsp.

- o Salt and pepper to taste

Directions:

Combine the mustard, honey, pepper, rosemary and salt in a bowl. Rub the chicken with this mixture.. Grease the air fryer basket with oil. Air fry the chicken at 350F for 20 to 24 minutes or until the chicken reaches 165F. Serve.

Chicken Parmesan Wings
Cook time: 15 minutes |Serves: 4| Per serving: Calories 490; Carbs 1g; Fat 22g; Protein 72g

Ingredients:

- Chicken wings – 2 lbs. cut into drumettes, pat dried
- Parmesan – ½ cup, plus 6 tbsps. grated
- Herbs de Provence – 1 tsp.
- Paprika – 1 tsp.
- Salt to taste

Directions:

Combine the parmesan, herbs, paprika, and salt in a bowl and rub the chicken with this mixture. Preheat the air fryer at 350F. Grease the basket with cooking spray. Cook for 15 minutes. Flip once at the halfway mark. Garnish with parmesan and serve.

Turkey Sausage Bake
Cook time: 30 minutes |Serves: 6| Per serving: Calories 320; Carbs 7g; Fat 20g; Protein 28g

Ingredients:

- Ground turkey sausage – 1 lb.
- Eggs - 6
- Half-and-half – ½ cup
- Cheddar cheese – ½ cup, shredded
- Broccoli – 1 small head, chopped into florets
- Red bell pepper – 1, diced
- Onion – 1, chopped
- Garlic – 2 cloves, chopped
- Olive oil – 1 tbsp.
- Salt and pepper to taste

Directions:

Heat the oil on Sauté. Sauté the sausage for 3 minutes. Add the onions and garlic and sauté for 2 minutes. Add the broccoli and red pepper and cook for 4 minutes. Then remove the mixture to a bowl. Crack the eggs in another bowl. add half-and-half, salt, and pepper then whisk to make it smooth. Grease ramekins and add about a quarter cup of the sausage mixture into each ramekin and cover with egg mixture. Sprinkle about 1 ½ tbsps. shredded cheddar cheese on top. Cook at 320F for 10 minutes. Cook in batches if necessary. Serve.

Southern-Style Chicken

Cook time: 30 minutes |Serves: 6| Per serving: Calories 403; Carbs 13g; Fat 23g; Protein 36g

Ingredients:

- Chicken – 4 lbs.
- Breadcrumbs – 2 cups
- Egg – 1, beaten
- Fresh parsley – 1 tbsp. minced
- Garlic salt – 1 tsp.
- Paprika – 1 tsp.
- Pepper – ½ tsp.
- Ground cumin – ¼ tsp.
- Sage – ¼ tsp.

Directions:

Preheat the air fryer to 375F and grease the basket with cooking spray. Mix the breadcrumbs, parsley, garlic salt, paprika, pepper, ground cumin, and sage in a bowl. Crack the egg in another bowl and whisk. Dip the chicken cuts into the egg then into the dry mixture. Cook the chicken in the air fryer for 10 minutes. Then flip and cook 10 to 20 minutes more or until golden brown. Serve.

Breaded Chicken

Cook time: 15 minutes |Serves: 4| Per serving: Calories 204; Carbs 5g; Fat 4g; Protein 37g

Ingredients:

- Boneless, skinless chicken breasts – 4, 6-oz. each
- Breadcrumbs – ¼ cup
- Garlic powder – 1/8 tsp.
- Paprika – 1/8 tsp.
- Oregano – ¼ tsp.
- Salt and pepper to taste

Directions:

Preheat the air fryer to 390F. Mix the garlic powder, breadcrumbs, and oregano in a bowl. Spray the chicken breasts with cooking spray then dredge them into the breadcrumb mixture and arrange them in the air fryer basket. Spray with cooking spray. Cook at 350F for 5 minutes. Then flip and spray with cooking spray. Cook for 5 minutes more. Serve.

Air Fryer Chicken
Cook time: 30 minutes |Serves: 4| Per serving: Calories 277; Carbs 1g; Fat 8g; Protein 50g

Ingredients:

- Chicken wings – 2 lbs.
- Salt and pepper to taste
- Cooking spray

Directions:

Season the chicken wings with salt and pepper. Spray the air fryer basket with cooking spray. Add chicken wings and cook at 400F for 35 minutes. Flip 3 times during cooking for even cooking. Serve.

Whole Chicken
Cook time: 45 minutes |Serves: 6| Per serving: Calories 412; Carbs 1g; Fat 28g; Protein 35g

Ingredients:

- Whole chicken – 1 (2 ½ pounds) washed and pat dried
- Dry rub – 2 tbsps.
- Salt – 1 tsp.
- Cooking spray

Directions:

Preheat the air fryer at 350F. Rub the dry rub on the chicken. Then rub with salt. Cook in the air fryer at 350F for 45 minutes. After 30 minutes, flip the chicken and finish cooking. Chicken is done when it reaches 165F.

Herb Turkey Breast

Cook time: 40 minutes |Serves: 6 | Per serving: Calories 406; Carbs 1g; Fat 26.5g; Protein 42g

Ingredients:

- Turkey breast with skin – 2 pounds
- Melted butter – 4 tbsps.
- Garlic – 3 cloves, grated
- Fresh rosemary – 1 tsp. chopped
- Thyme – 1 tsp. chopped
- Ground black pepper – 1 tsp.
- Salt to taste
- Cooking spray

Directions:

Rub the turkey with salt and pepper. Combine rosemary, butter, thyme, and garlic in a bowl. Rub the turkey with this mixture. Grease the air fryer with cooking spray. Cook the turkey for 40 minutes at 375F. After 20 minutes, flip the turkey breast and spray with cooking oil. Finish cooking. Serve.

Garlic Parmesan Chicken

Cook time: 20 minutes |Serves: 4| Per serving: Calories 614; Carbs 13g; Fat 41g; Protein 46g

Ingredients:

- Chicken thighs – 2 pounds, with bone and skin
- Eggs – 2
- Shredded parmesan - ¾ cup
- Panko breadcrumbs – 1 cup
- Italian seasoning – tsp.
- Garlic powder – 1 tsp.
- Salt and pepper to taste
- Cooking spray

Directions:

Rub chicken with salt and pepper. Combine panko breadcrumbs, Italian seasoning, garlic powder, grated parmesan in a bowl. Beats eggs in a bowl. Dip the chicken in the egg and then in the bread mixture. Cook in the air fryer at 400F for 20 minutes. Flip at the halfway mark. Serve.

Thanksgiving Turkey

Cook time: 37 minutes |Serves: 4| Per serving: Calories 442; Carbs 15g; Fat 19g; Protein 50g

Ingredients:

- o   Turkey breast – 2 pounds
- o   Chopped thyme – 1 tsp.
- o   Chopped rosemary – 1 tsp.
- o   Maple syrup – ¼ cup
- o   Chopped sage – 1 tsp.
- o   Dijon mustard – 2 tbsps.
- o   Butter – 1 tbsp.
- o   Salt and pepper to taste
- o   Cooking spray

Directions:

Rub the turkey with salt and pepper. Rub thyme, rosemary, and sage on the turkey breasts. Combine butter, mustard, maple syrup in a bowl. Grease the air fryer basket with cooking spray. Cook the turkey in the air fryer for 35 minutes at 390F. Flip once at the halfway mark. Then remove the turkey and brush it with maple syrup sauce. Cook again for 2 minutes at 330F. Serve.

Turkey Burgers

Cook time: 16 minutes |Serves: 4| Per serving: Calories 200; Carbs 0g; Fat 12g; Protein 12g

Ingredients:

- o   Turkey meat – 1 pound, ground
- o   Shallot – 1 minced
- o   A drizzle of olive oil
- o   Small jalapeno pepper – 1, minced

- o Lime juice – 2 tsps.

- o Zest from 1 lime, grated

- o Salt and black pepper to taste

- o Cumin – 1 tsp. ground

- o Sweet paprika – 1 tsp.

- o Guacamole for serving

Directions:

In a bowl, mix turkey meat with lime juice, zest, jalapeno, shallot, paprika, cumin, salt, and pepper. Mix well. Shape burgers from this mix and drizzle the oil over them. Cook in the preheated air fryer at 370F for 8 minutes on each side. Divide among plates and serve with guacamole on top.

Honey Duck Breasts

Cook time: 22 minutes |Serves: 2| Per serving: Calories 274; Carbs 22g; Fat 11g; Protein 13g

Ingredients:

- o Smoked duck breast – 1, halved

- o Honey – 1 tsp.

- o Tomato paste – 1 tsp.

- o Mustard – 1 tbsp.

- o Apple vinegar – ½ tsp.

Directions:

Mix tomato paste, honey, mustard, and vinegar in a bowl. Whisk well. Add duck breast pieces and coat well. Cook in the air fryer at 370F for 15 minutes. Remove the duck breast from the air fryer and add to the honey mixture. Coat again. Cook again at 370F for 6 minutes. Serve.

Chinese Duck Legs

Cook time: 36 minutes |Serves: 2| Per serving: Calories 300; Carbs 26g; Fat 12g; Protein 18g

Ingredients:

- o Duck legs – 2

- o Dried chilies – 2, chopped

- o Olive oil – 1 tbsp.

- o Star anise – 2

- o Spring onions – 1 bunch, chopped

- o Ginger – 4 slices

- o Oyster sauce – 1 tbsp.

- o Soy sauce – 1 tbsp.

- o Sesame oil – 1 tsp.

- o Water – 14 ounces

- o Rice wine – 1 tbsp.

Directions:

Heat oil in a pan. Add water, soy sauce, oyster sauce, ginger, rice wine, sesame oil, star anise, and chili. Stir and cook for 6 minutes. Add spring onions and duck legs, toss to coat and transfer to a pan. Place the pan in the air fryer and cook at 370F for 30 minutes. Serve.

Duck Breasts with Endives
Cook time: 25 minutes |Serves: 4| Per serving: Calories 400; Carbs 29g; Fat 12g; Protein 28g

Ingredients:

- o Duck breasts – 2

- o Salt and black pepper to taste

- o Sugar – 1 tbsp.

- o Olive oil – 1 tbsp.

- o Endives – 6, julienned

- o Cranberries – 2 tbsps.

- o White wine – 8 ounces

- o Garlic – 1 tbsp. minced

- o Heavy cream – 2 tbsps.

Directions:

Score duck breasts and season with salt and pepper. Cook in the air fryer at 350F for 20 minutes. Flip once. Meanwhile, heat up a pan with oil over medium heat. Add endives, and sugar. Stir and cook for 2 minutes. Add salt, pepper, wine, garlic, cream, and cranberries — Stir-Fry for 3 minutes. Divide duck breasts on plates. Drizzle with the endives sauce and serve.

Creamy Coconut Chicken
Cook time: 25 minutes |Serves: 4| Per serving: Calories 300; Carbs 22g; Fat 4g; Protein 20g

Ingredients:

- Big chicken legs – 4
- Turmeric powder – 5 tsps.
- Ginger – 2 tbsps. grated
- Salt and black pepper to taste
- Coconut cream – 4 tbsps.

Directions:

In a bowl, mix salt, pepper, ginger, turmeric, and cream. Whisk. Add chicken pieces, coat and marinate for 2 hours. Transfer chicken to the preheated air fryer and cook at 370F for 25 minutes. Serve.

Chinese Chicken Wings
Cook time: 15 minutes |Serves: 6| Per serving: Calories 372; Carbs 37g; Fat 9g; Protein 24g

Ingredients:

- Chicken wings – 16
- Honey – 2 tbsps.
- Soy sauce – 2 tbsps.
- Salt and black pepper to taste
- White pepper – ¼ tsp.
- Lime juice – 3 tbsps.

Directions:

In a bowl, mix soy sauce, honey, salt, black pepper, lime juice, and white pepper. Whisk well. Add chicken pieces and coat well. Marinate in the refrigerator for 2 hours. Then cook in the air fryer at 370F for 6 minutes on each side. Then increase heat to 400F and cook for 3 minutes more. Serve.

Herbed Chicken
Cook time: 40 minutes |Serves: 4| Per serving: Calories 390; Carbs 22g; Fat 10g; Protein 20g

Ingredients:

- o   Whole chicken – 1
- o   Salt and black pepper to taste
- o   Garlic powder – 1 tsp.
- o   Onion powder – 1 tsp.
- o   Thyme – ½ tsp. dried
- o   Rosemary – 1 tsp. dried
- o   Lemon juice – 1 tbsp.
- o   Olive oil – 2 tbsps.

Directions:

Season chicken with salt and pepper. Rub with onion powder, garlic powder, rosemary, and thyme. Rub with olive oil and lemon juice and marinate for 30 minutes. Cook chicken in the air fryer at 360F for 20 minutes on each side. Carve and serve.

Chicken Parmesan
Cook time: 15 minutes |Serves: 4| Per serving: Calories 304; Carbs 22g; Fat 12g; Protein 15g

Ingredients:

- o   Panko bread crumbs – 2 cups
- o   Parmesan – ¼ cup, grated
- o   Garlic powder – ½ tsp.
- o   White flour – 2 cups
- o   Egg – 1, whisked
- o   Chicken cutlets – 1 ½ pounds, skinless, and boneless

- o Salt and pepper to taste

- o Mozzarella - 1 cup, grated

- o Tomato sauce – 2 cups

- o Basil – 3 tbsps. chopped

Directions:

In a bowl, mix garlic powder, and parmesan and stir. Put flour in a second bowl and the egg in a third. Season chicken with salt, and pepper. Dip in flour, then in the egg mix and in panko. Cook chicken pieces in the air fryer at 360F for 3 minutes on each side. Transfer chicken to a baking dish. Add tomato sauce, and top with mozzarella. Cook in the air fryer at 375F for 7 minutes. Divide among plates, sprinkle basil on top and serve.

Mexican Chicken
Cook time: 22 minutes |Serves: 4| Per serving: Calories 340; Carbs 32g; Fat 18g; Protein 18g

Ingredients:

- o Salsa verde – 16 ounces

- o Olive oil – 1 tbsp.

- o Salt and black pepper to taste

- o Chicken breast – 1 pound, boneless, and skinless

- o Monetary Jack cheese – 1 ½ cups, grated

- o Cilantro – ¼ cup, chopped

- o Garlic powder – 1 tsp.

Directions:

Pour salsa verde in a baking dish. Season chicken with garlic powder, salt, pepper, and brush with olive oil. Place over the salsa verde. Place in the air fryer and cook at 380F for 20 minutes. Sprinkle cheese on top and cook 2 minutes more. Serve.

Italian Chicken
Cook time: 16 minutes |Serves: 4| Per serving: Calories 272; Carbs 37g; Fat 9g; Protein 23g

Ingredients:

- o Chicken thighs – 8

- o Olive oil – 1 tbsp.

- o Garlic – 2 cloves, minced

- o Thyme - 1 tbsp. chopped

- o Heavy cream – ½ cup

- o Chicken stock - ¾ cup

- o Red pepper flakes – 1 tsp. crushed

- o Parmesan – ¼ cup, grated

- o Sun-dried tomatoes – ½ cup

- o Basil – 2 tbsps. chopped

- o Salt and black pepper to taste

Directions:

Season chicken with salt and pepper, and rub with half of the oil. Place in the preheated air fryer at 350F and cook for 4 minutes. Meanwhile, heat the rest of the oil in a pan and add garlic, thyme, pepper flakes, tomatoes, stock, heavy cream, salt, parmesan, and pepper. Bring to a simmer and remove from the heat. Place the mixture in a dish. Add chicken thighs on top and cook in the air fryer at 320F for 12 minutes. Serve with basil sprinkled on top.

Chicken Salad
Cook time: 10 minutes |Serves: 4| Per serving: Calories 312; Carbs 22g; Fat 6g; Protein 26g

Ingredients:

- o Chicken breast – 1 pound, boneless, skinless and halved

- o Cooking spray

- o Salt and black pepper to taste

- o Feta cheese – ½ cup, cubed

- o Lemon juice – 2 tbsps.

- o Mustard – 1 ½ tsps.

- o Olive oil – 1 tbsp.

- o Red wine vinegar – 1 ½ tsps.

- o   Anchovies – ½ tsp. minced

- o   Garlic – ¾ tsp. minced

- o   Water – 1 tbsp.

- o   Lettuce leaves – 8 cups, cut into strips

- o   Parmesan – 4 tbsps. grated

Directions:

Spray chicken breasts with cooking oil. Season with salt and pepper. Place in the air fryer and cook at 370F for 10 minutes. Flip once. Shred the chicken with 2 forks. Put in a salad bowl and mix with lettuce leaves. In the blender, mix feta cheese with lemon juice, olive oil, mustard, vinegar, garlic, anchovies, water and half of the parmesan and blend very well. Add this over the chicken mix. Toss and sprinkle the rest of the parmesan and serve.

Buffalo Chicken Tenders

Cook time: 20 minutes |Serves: 4 | Per serving: Calories 160; Carbs 0.6g; Fat 4.4g; Protein 27.3g

Ingredients:

- o   Boneless, skinless chicken tenders – 1 pound

- o   Hot sauce – ¼ cup

- o   Pork rinds – 1 ½ ounces, finely ground

- o   Chili powder – 1 tsp.

- o   Garlic powder – 1 tsp.

Directions:

Place chicken breasts in a bowl and pour hot sauce over them. Toss to coat. Mix ground pork rinds, chili powder and garlic powder in another bowl. Place each tender in the ground pork rinds, and coat well. With wet hands, press down the pork rinds into the chicken. Place the tender in a single layer into the air fryer basket. Cook at 375F for 20 minutes. Flip once. Serve.

Teriyaki Wings

Cook time: 25 minutes |Serves: 4| Per serving: Calories 446; Carbs 3.1g; Fat 29.8g; Protein 41.8g

Ingredients:

- o   Chicken wings – 2 pounds

- o Teriyaki sauce – ½ cup

- o Minced garlic – 2 tsp.

- o Ground ginger - ¼ tsp.

- o Baking powder – 2 tsp.

Directions:

Except for the baking powder, place all ingredients in a bowl and marinate for 1 hour in the refrigerator. Place wings into the air fryer basket and sprinkle with baking powder. Gently rub into wings. Cook at 400F for 25 minutes. Shake the basket two or three times during cooking. Serve.

Lemony Drumsticks

Cook time: 25 minutes |Serves: 2| Per serving: Calories 532; Carbs 1.2g; Fat 32.3g; Protein 48.3g

Ingredients:

- o Baking powder – 2 tsps.

- o Garlic powder – ½ tsp.

- o Chicken drumsticks – 8

- o Salted butter – 4 tbsps. melted

- o Lemon pepper seasoning – 1 tbsp.

Directions:

Sprinkle garlic powder and baking powder over drumsticks and rub into chicken skin. Place drumsticks into the air fryer basket. Cook at 375F for 25 minutes. Flip the drumsticks once halfway through the cooking time. Remove when cooked. Mix seasoning and butter in a bowl. Add drumsticks to the bowl and toss to coat. Serve.

Coconut Shrimp

Cook time: 15 minutes |Serves: 2| Per serving: Calories 406; Carbs 48.4g; Fat 9.2g; Protein 32.4g

Ingredients:

- ○ Flour – ½ cup
- ○ Kosher Salt – 1 tsp.
- ○ Breadcrumbs – ¾ cup
- ○ Shredded unsweetened coconut – ½ cup
- ○ White pepper – ½ tsp.
- ○ Egg whites – 2, lightly beaten
- ○ Shrimp – 1 pound, peeled and deveined
- ○ Sweet chili sauce to taste
- ○ Lime zest – 2 tsps.
- ○ Salt – 1 tsp.

Directions:

Combine flour, kosher salt, and white pepper in a bowl. Add egg whites to a second bowl. Combine breadcrumbs, coconut, lime zest, and salt in a third bowl. Dip the shrimp in the flour mixture, then in the egg mixture and lastly in the breadcrumb mixture. Coat well. Cook 12 minutes at 400F in the air fryer. Flip the shrimp after 5 minutes. Serve.

Baked Shrimp Scampi

Cook time: 10 minutes |Serves: 4| Per serving: Calories 422; Carbs 18g; Fat 26g; Protein 29g

Ingredients:

o   Large shrimp – 1 lb.

o   Butter – 8 tbsps.

o   Minced garlic – 1 tbsp.

o   White wine – ¼ cup

o   Salt – ½ tsp.

o   Cayenne pepper – ¼ tsp.

o   Paprika – ¼ tsp.

o   Onion powder – ½ tsp.

o   Bread crumbs – ¾ cup

Directions:

Mix bread crumbs with dry seasonings in a bowl. Melt the butter on Sauté with garlic and white wine. Remove from the heat and add the shrimp and bread crumb mix. Transfer this mix to a casserole dish. Choose the Bake option and add food to the air fryer. Cook at 350F for 10 minutes. Serve.

Marinated Salmon

Cook time: 12 minutes |Serves: 4| Per serving: Calories 267; Carbs 5g; Fat 11g; Protein 37g

Ingredients:

o   Salmon – 4 fillets

o   Brown sugar – 1 tbsp.

o   Minced garlic – ½ tbsp.

o   Soy sauce – 6 tbsps.

o   Dijon mustard – ¼ cup

o   Chopped green onion – 1

Directions:

In a bowl, mix mustard, soy sauce, brown sugar, and minced garlic. Pour this mixture over salmon fillets and coat well. Marinate for 30 minutes in the refrigerator. Then cook in the air fryer at 400F for 12 minutes. Garnish with green onions and serve.

Coconut Shrimp
Cook time: 9 minutes |Serves: 4| Per serving: Calories 279; Carbs 17g; Fat 11g; Protein 28g

Ingredients:

- Large raw shrimp - 1 lb. peeled and deveined with tail on
- Eggs – 2, beaten
- Panko breadcrumbs – ¼ cup
- Salt – 1 tsp.
- Black pepper to taste
- Flour – ½ cup
- Unsweetened shredded coconut – ½ cup
- Cooking spray

Directions:

Take 3 bowls. Put flour in the first, and beaten eggs in the second. Mix Breadcrumbs, coconut, salt and black pepper in the third bowl. Preheat the air fryer to 390F. Dip shrimp in flour, then in egg and then in the breadcrumb mixture. Coat well. Place in the air fryer and spray with oil. Cook in the air fryer for 4 minutes. Then flip and spray again. Cook for 5 minutes more. Serve.

Air Fryer Fish
Cook time: 17 minutes |Serves: 4| Per serving: Calories 193; Carbs 27g; Fat 1g; Protein 19g

Ingredients:

- Whitefish fillets - 4
- Cooking spray

Fish seasoning

- Very fine cornmeal – ¾ cup
- Flour – ¼ cup
- Old bay seasoning – 2 tsps.
- Salt – 1 ½ tsps.
- Paprika – 1 tsp.

- Garlic powder – ½ tsp.
- Black pepper – ½ tsp.

Directions:

Put the ingredients for fish seasoning in a Ziplock bag and shake well. Set aside. Place the fish fillets in the Ziplock bag and shake well to coat. Grease the air fryer basket with cooking spray. Cook the fillets for 10 minutes at 400F. Open and spray the fish with oil. Then flip and cook for 7 minutes more. Serve.

Lobster Tails

Cook time: 8 minutes |Serves: 2| Per serving: Calories 120; Carbs 2g; Fat 12g; Protein 1g

Ingredients:

- Lobster tails – 2 (6 oz.) butterflied
- Salt – 1 tsp.
- Chopped chives – 1 tsp.
- Unsalted butter – 2 tbsps. melted
- Minced garlic -1 tbsp.
- Lemon juice – 1 tsp.

Directions:

Combine garlic, butter, salt, chives, and lemon juice. Spread the lobster tails with butter mix and cook in the air fryer at 380F for 4 minutes. Then open and spread more butter on top. Cook for 2 to 4 minutes more. Serve.

Crispy-Fried Salmon

Cook time:10 minutes |Serves: 2|Per serving: Calories 317; Carbs 10.33g; Fat 14.38g;Protein 36.66g

Ingredients:

- Thyme – ½ tsp.
- Brown sugar – 1 tsp.
- Whole grain mustard – 2 tbsps.
- Black pepper to taste
- Salmon fillets – 2 (6 oz. each)

- o Olive oil – 2 tsps.
- o Garlic – 1 clove, minced

Directions:

Rub the salmon with salt and pepper. In a bowl, mix the garlic, mustard, sugar, thyme, and oil. Whisk to blend. Spread the mixture on top of the salmon. Cook in the air fryer at 400F for 10 minutes. Flip once at the halfway mark. Serve.

Tuna Patties
Cook time: 10 minutes |Serves: 10| Per serving: Calories 119; Carbs 5; Fat 4.8g; Protein 13.4g

Ingredients:

- o Dried herbs – ½ tsp.
- o Eggs – 2
- o Tuna in a can – 15 oz., drained
- o Zest of 1 medium lemon
- o Black pepper to taste
- o Bread crumbs – ½ cup
- o Lemon juice – 1 tbsp.
- o Grated parmesan cheese – 3 tbsps.
- o Onion – 3 tbsps. chopped
- o Celery – 1 stalk, chopped
- o Garlic powder – ½ tsp.
- o Kosher salt to taste

Directions:

Combine parmesan cheese, eggs, breadcrumbs, lemon zest, garlic powder, onion, celery, and dried herbs in a bowl. Season with salt and pepper. Fold in the tuna and stir to mix. Make about 10 patties. Line the air fryer basket with parchment paper and spray with cooking spray. Add the patties and spray with cooking spray. Cook for 10 minutes at 360F. Flip at the halfway mark and spray with cooking spray. Serve.

Garlic-Lemon Shrimp

Cook time: 15 minutes |Serves: 2| Per serving: Calories 243; Carbs 4.11g; Fat 4.34g; Protein 46.93g

Ingredients:

- Raw shrimp – 1 lb. peeled and deveined
- Garlic powder – ¼ tsp.
- Lemon wedges to taste
- Cooking spray
- Salt and pepper to taste
- Parsley – 1 tbsp. minced
- Chili flakes to taste

Directions:

Add shrimp in a bowl. Add oil and mix. Add garlic powder, and season with salt and pepper. Mix well. Cook in the air fryer at 400F for 10 to 14 minutes. Flip once at the halfway mark. Then remove and squeeze over lemon juice. Sprinkle with chili flakes and parsley and serve.

Whitefish with Garlic and Lemon

Cook time: 10 minutes |Serves: 2| Per serving: Calories 308; Carbs 6.88g; Fat 16.47g; Protein 33g

Ingredients:

- Salt and pepper to taste
- Lemon pepper seasoning – ½ tsp.
- Whitefish fillets – 12 oz.
- Chopped parsley to taste
- Garlic powder – ½ tsp.
- Lemon wedges to taste
- Onion powder – ½ tsp.

Directions:

Coat the fish with oil. Season with onion powder, garlic powder, and lemon pepper. Then season with salt and pepper. Coat well. Line the air fryer basket with parchment and spray with oil.

Arrange fish and add a few lemon wedges. Cook at 360F for 6 to 12 minutes or until fish is cooked. Flip once at the halfway mark. Serve.

Shrimps with Lemon

Cook time: 15 minutes |Serves: 2 | Per serving: Calories 117; Carbs 2g; Fat 1.66g; Protein 23.46g

Ingredients:

- o   Garlic powder – ¼ tsp.
- o   Raw shrimps -1 pound, peeled and deveined
- o   Oil as needed
- o   Chopped parsley to taste
- o   Black pepper and salt to taste
- o   Lemon wedges to serve

Directions:

In a bowl, combine shrimp with oil, salt, pepper and garlic. Mix well. Place shrimps in the air fryer basket and cook at 400F for 10 to 14 minutes. Flip the shrimp at the halfway mark. Drizzle shrimp with lemon juice and serve.

Crumbled Fish

Cook time: 12 minutes |Serves: 4| Per serving: Calories 357; Carbs 22.5g; Fat 17.7g; Protein 26.9g

Ingredients:

- o   Oil – ¼ cup
- o   Egg – 1, beaten
- o   Flounder fillets – 4
- o   Dry bread crumbs – 1 cup
- o   Lemon – 1 sliced

Directions:

In a bowl, mix oil and bread crumbs. Dredge fillets into the egg, then into the bread crumbs to coat well. Cook in the air fryer at 350F for 12 minutes. Flip at the halfway mark of the cooking. Garnish with lemon slices and serve.

Coconut Shrimp

Cook time: 15 minutes |Serves: 6| Per serving: Calories 247; Carbs 27.6g; Fat 9.1g; Protein 13.8g

Ingredients:

- Eggs – 2
- Salt and pepper to taste
- Panko breadcrumbs – 3 cups
- All-purpose flour – ½ cup
- Honey – ¼ cup
- Flaked coconut – 3 cups, unsweetened
- Shrimps – 12 oz. raw, peeled and deveined
- Serrano chili – 1, sliced
- Fresh cilantro – 2 tsps.
- Lime juice – ¼ cup

Directions:

Combine flour and pepper in a bowl. Lightly beat the eggs in another bowl. Add coconut and breadcrumbs in the third bowl. Dredge shrimps in the flour, then in the eggs, and in the breadcrumbs mixture. Coat well. Line the air fryer basket with parchment paper. Coat shrimps with cooking spray. Cook at 200F for 3 minutes. Then flip and cook for another 3 minutes. Cook in batches if necessary. Season with salt. Combine honey and serrano chili with lime juice in a bowl. Serve shrimp with the dip.

Fish Sticks

Cook time: 10 minutes |Serves: 4| Per serving: Calories 208; Carbs 16.5g; Fat 4.1g; Protein 26.3g

Ingredients:

- All-purpose flour – ½ cup
- Whitefish fillet – 1 lb. cut into 1x3 inch sticks
- Egg – 1, beaten
- Parmesan cheese – ½ cup, grated

- o   Panko bread crumbs – ½ cup

- o   Paprika – 1 tsp.

- o   Parsley flakes – 1 tbsp.

- o   Black pepper -1 tsp.

- o   Cooking spray

Directions:

Take 3 bowls. Put flour in the first bowl. Beaten egg in the second bowl and mix parmesan, panko bread crumbs, and seasoning in the third bowl. Coat fish sticks with flour, then dip in the egg and lastly dip in the seasoned bread crumbs. Coat well. Line the air fryer basket with parchment and spray with cooking oil. Cook the fish sticks at 400F for 5 minutes. Then flip the fish stick and cook for 5 minutes more. Serve.

Lobster Tails with Lemon-Garlic Butter
Cook time: 10 minutes |Serves: 2| Per serving: Calories 418; Carbs 3.3g; Fat 25.8g; Protein 18g

Ingredients:

- o   Butter – 4 tbsps.

- o   Lobster tails – 2 (4-oz.) butterflied

- o   Lemon zest – 1 tsp.

- o   Chopped parsley – 1 tsp.

- o   Garlic – 1 clove, minced

- o   Lemon – 2 wedges

- o   Salt and black pepper to taste

Directions:

Add lobster tails in the air fryer basket with lobster meat facing upward. Add lemon zest, butter, and garlic in the Instant Pot and Sauté for 30 seconds. Then transfer 2 tbsps. of butter mixture to the small bowl and brush onto the lobster. Season lobster with salt and pepper. Place the air fryer basket in the air fryer. Cover and cook at 380F for 5 to 7 minutes. Serve lobster with melted butter, parsley and lemon wedge.

Air Fried Shrimps
Cook time: 10 minutes |Serves: 4| Per serving: Calories 122; Carbs 0.5g; Fat 4.6g; Protein 19.6g

Ingredients:

- o   Large shrimps - 1 lb. peeled and deveined
- o   Butter – 1 tbsp.
- o   Garlic – ½ tsp.
- o   Lemon juice -1 tsp.
- o   Parmesan cheese – 1/8 cup, grated
- o   Salt – 1/8 tsp.

Directions:

Remove shrimps' tails. Mix in lemon, garlic, and salt to a bowl with melted butter. Add shrimps and coat well. Line air fryer basket with parchment paper, grease with cooking spray and place in shrimps. Spray with cooking spray and cook for 8 minutes at 400F. Flip at the halfway mark and spray with cooking spray. Finish cooking and serve.

Shrimp with Bang Bang Sauce
Cook time: 24 minutes |Serves: 4| Per serving: Calories 442; Carbs 32g; Fat 23g; Protein 23g

Ingredients:

- o   Raw shrimp – 1 lb. peeled and deveined
- o   Mayonnaise – ½ cup
- o   Sriracha sauce – 1 tbsp.
- o   Sweet chili sauce – ¼ cup
- o   Lettuce – 1 head
- o   All-purpose flour – ¼ cup
- o   Green onions – 2 chopped
- o   Panko bread crumbs – 1 cup

Directions:

To make the sauce, add chili sauce, mayonnaise, and sriracha sauce in a bowl and whisk until smooth. Place flour in a bowl and panko breadcrumbs on another dish. Coat shrimp with flour then with the breadcrumbs. Line air fryer basket with parchment and grease with cooking spray. Cook shrimp for 12 minutes at 500F. Flip at the halfway mark spray cooking oil. Finish cooking. Serve with lettuce and green onions.

Cajun Salmon
Cook time: 10 minutes |Serves: 2| Per serving: Calories 122; Carbs 0.5g; Fat 4.6g; Protein 19.6g

Ingredients:

- o Salmon fillet – 2 (6 oz. each) with skin
- o Brown sugar – 1 tsp.
- o Cajun seasoning – 1 tbsp.
- o Cooking spray

Directions:

In a bowl, combine seasoning and sugar. Dip fillets into the mixture and coat well. Grease the air fryer basket with cooking spray and place the fillets on it, skin-side down. Spray with cooking spray and cook at 390F for 8 minutes. Serve.

Lemon Garlic Shrimp
Cook time: 5 minutes |Serves: 4| Per serving: Calories 120; Carbs 3g; Fat 4.6g; Protein 16g

Ingredients:

- o Shrimp – 1 pound
- o Garlic – 4 cloves, chopped
- o Crushed red pepper flakes – ¼ tsp.
- o Oil – 1 tbsp.
- o Juice and zest of 1 lemon
- o Parsley – ¼ cup, chopped
- o Salt to taste

Directions:

Peel, devein, and remove the tails of the shrimps. Place minced garlic, lemon zest, shrimps, red pepper flakes, salt, and oil in a bowl. Mix. Preheat the air fryer at 400F. Coat the shrimps in the garlic mixture. Cook in the air fryer for 5 minutes at 400F. Flip the shrimp at the halfway mark. Finish cooking. Drizzle with lemon juice and garnish with chopped parsley.

Fish and Chips
Cook time: 15 minutes |Serves: 4| Per serving: Calories 338; Carbs 12g; Fat 17g; Protein 35g

Ingredients:

- o   Cod fillets – 1 ¼ lbs.

- o   Eggs – 2, beaten

- o   Almond flour – 1 cup

- o   Garlic powder – ½ tsp.

- o   Onion powder – ½ tsp.

- o   Dried parsley – 1 tbsp.

- o   Arrowroot powder – 1 tbsp.

- o   Salt to taste

Directions:

Combine the parsley, almond flour, onion powder, salt, arrowroot powder, and garlic powder in a bowl. Dip the fish fillets in the beaten eggs, then in the almond flour mix. Grease the air fryer basket with cooking spray and place the fish in the basket. Grease with oil. Cook at 350F for 14 minutes. Flip the fillets at the halfway mark. Serve.

Air Fryer Salmon
Cook time: 15 minutes |Serves: 2| Per serving: Calories 202; Carbs 7g; Fat 11g; Protein 18g

Ingredients:

- o   Salmon fillets – 2 (6 ounces) fillets

- o   Olive oil – 2 tsps.

- o   Ground black pepper – ½ tsp.

- o   Mustard – 2 tbsps.

- o   Garlic – 1 clove, chopped

- o   Brown sugar -1 tbsp.

o   Thyme leaves – ½ tsp.

Directions:

Rub the salmon with salt and pepper. Combine thyme, mustard, garlic, brown sugar, and oil in a bowl. Rub this mix on the salmon. Cook the salmon in the air fryer at 400F for 10 minutes. Flip at the halfway mark. Serve.

Fish Finger Sandwich
Cook time: 15 minutes |Serves: 4| Per serving: Calories 458; Carbs 44g; Fat 18.8g; Protein 29g

Ingredients:

o   Cod fillet – 13 ounces, skin removed

o   Flour – 2 tbsps.

o   Breadcrumbs -1 ½ ounces

o   Capers – 12

o   Frozen peas – 10 ounces

o   Greek yogurt -1 tbsp.

o   Lemon juice – 1 tbsp.

o   Bread – 8 small slices

o   Salt and pepper to taste

o   Cooking oil spray

Directions:

Preheat the air fryer to 390F. Rub the fillet with salt and pepper. Place flour and breadcrumbs in separate bowls. Then coat the fillets in flour and in breadcrumbs. Spray with cooking oil and place in the air fryer. Cook at 390F for 15 minutes. Flip once at the halfway mark. Meanwhile. Boil the peas for 5 minutes or until tender. Then drain and put them in a blender. Add capers, yogurt, and lemon juice. Mix. Arrange the sandwich with bread, fish and pea puree. Serve.

Tuna Patties
Cook time: 6 minutes |Serves: 4 | Per serving: Calories 67; Carbs 2g; Fat 1.8g; Protein 11g

Ingredients:

o   Canned tuna – 7 ounces

- o   Egg – 1

- o   Breadcrumbs – ¼ cup

- o   Mustard – 1 tbsp.

- o   Salt and pepper to taste

- o   Cooking spray

Directions:

Combine egg, tuna, bread crumbs, salt, pepper and mustard in a bowl. Make four patties with this mixture. Grease the air fryer basket with cooking oil. Cook the patties in Broil setting for 6 minutes. Flip the patties after 3 minutes. Serve.

Grilled Cod with Sauce

Cook time: 10 minutes |Serves: 2| Per serving: Calories 657; Carbs 15g; Fat 54g; Protein 29g

Ingredients:

- o   Cod fillets – 1 pound

- o   Olive oil – 2 tbsps.

- o   Lemon juice – 1 tbsp.

- o   Salt and pepper to taste

Sauce

- o   Heavy cream – ½ cup
- o   Ground mustard – 3 tbsps.
- o   Butter – 1 tbsp.
- o   Salt to taste

Directions:

Spread some oil on the fillets. Rub salt, pepper, and lemon juice on the fillets. Grease the air fryer basket and cook the fillets at 350F for 5 minutes. Then flip the fish and increase the temperature to 400F and cook for 5 minutes more. Meanwhile, add all the sauce ingredients in a saucepan and cook for 4 minutes or until thick. Serve cod with sauce.

Ranch Air Fryer Fish Fillets

Cook time: 12 minutes |Serves: 4| Per serving: Calories 315; Carbs 8g; Fat 14g; Protein 38g

Ingredients:

- Tilapia fillets – 24 ounces
- Dry ranch-style dressing mix – 5 ounces
- Panko breadcrumbs – ¾ cup
- Eggs - 2
- Oil – 2 ½ tbsps.
- Lemon wedges- 4

Directions:

Mix the ranch dressing and breadcrumbs in a bowl. Add oil and mix again. Preheat the air fryer. Beat the eggs in a bowl. Dip the fillet in the egg mix then in the breadcrumbs. Coat well. Cook the fish in the air fryer at 360F for 12 minutes. Flip the fish at the halfway mark. Serve with lemon wedges.

Tasty Cod

Cook time: 12 minutes |Serves: 4| Per serving: Calories 300; Carbs 20g; Fat 17g; Protein 22g

Ingredients:

- Cod fillets – 2 (7-ounce) each
- Sesame oil – 1 drizzle
- Salt and black pepper to taste
- Water – 1 cup
- Dark soy sauce – 1 tsp.
- Light soy sauce – 4 tbsps.
- Sugar – 1 tbsp.
- Olive oil – 3 tbsps.
- Ginger – 4 slices
- Spring onions – 3, chopped
- Coriander – 2 tbsps. chopped

Directions:

Season fish with sesame oil, salt, and pepper. Rub well and leave aside for 10 minutes. Cook in the air-fryer at 356F for 12 minutes. Meanwhile, heat up a pot with water over medium heat. Add both soy sauces, and sugar, stir and bring to a simmer. Take off heat. Heat olive oil in a pan over medium heat. Add green onions, and ginger, stir, and cook for a few minutes and take off the heat. Divide fish on plates, top with green onions, and ginger. Drizzle with soy sauce mix, sprinkle coriander. Serve.

Delicious Catfish
Cook time: 20 minutes |Serves: 4| Per serving: Calories 253; Carbs 26g; Fat 6g; Protein 22g

Ingredients:

- o   Catfish fillets – 4
- o   Salt and black pepper to taste
- o   A pinch of sweet paprika
- o   Parsley – 1 tbsp. chopped
- o   Lemon juice – 1 tbsp.
- o   Olive oil – 1 tbsp.

Directions:

Season catfish fillets with oil, paprika, pepper, and salt. Rub well. Cook in the air-fryer at 400F for 20 minutes. Flip the fish after 10 minutes. Divide fish on plates, drizzle lemon juice all over, sprinkle parsley and serve.

Tabasco Shrimp
Cook time: 10 minutes |Serves: 4| Per serving: Calories 200; Carbs 13g; Fat 5g; Protein 8g

Ingredients:

- o   Shrimp – 1 pound, peeled and deveined
- o   Red pepper flakes – 1 tsp.
- o   Olive oil – 2 tbsps.
- o   Tabasco sauce – 1 tsp.
- o   Water – 2 tbsps.
- o   Oregano – 1 tsp. dried

- o Salt and black pepper to taste

- o Dried parsley – ½ tsp.

- o Smoked paprika – ½ tsp.

Directions:

In a bowl, mix water, oil, Tabasco sauce, shrimp, paprika, pepper, salt, parsley, oregano, and pepper flakes. Coat well. Transfer shrimp to preheated air fryer at 370F and cook for 10 minutes. Shake once. Serve.

Buttered Shrimp Skewers
Cook time: 6 minutes |Serves: 2| Per serving: Calories 140; Carbs 15g; Fat 1g; Protein 7g

Ingredients:

- o Shrimps – 8, peeled and deveined

- o Garlic – 4 cloves, minced

- o Salt and black pepper to taste

- o Green bell pepper slices – 8

- o Rosemary – 1 tbsp. chopped

- o Butter – 1 tbsp. melted

Directions:

In a bowl, mix bell pepper slices, rosemary, pepper, salt, butter, garlic, and shrimp. Toss to coat and marinate for 10 minutes. Arrange 2 bell pepper slices and 2 shrimp on a skewer and repeat with the rest of the shrimp and bell pepper pieces. Cook them at 360F for 6 minutes. Serve.

Asian Salmon
Cook time: 15 minutes |Serves: 2| Per serving: Calories 300; Carbs 13g; Fat 12g; Protein 24g

Ingredients:

- o Salmon fillets – 2 medium

- o Light soy sauce – 6 tbsps.

- o Mirin – 3 tbsps.

- o Water – 1 tsp.

- o Honey – 6 tbsps.

Directions:

Mix soy sauce with water, honey, mirin and whisk well. Add salmon, rub well and marinate in the fridge for 1 hour. Cook at 360F for 15 minutes in the air-fryer. Flip once after 7 minutes. Meanwhile, put the soy marinade in a pan, and simmer and whisk on medium heat for 2 minutes. Divide salmon on plates. Drizzle marinade all over and serve.

Air Fried Salmon

Cook time: 8 minutes |Serves: 2 | Per serving: Calories 300; Carbs 23g; Fat 12g; Protein 20g

Ingredients:

- Salmon fillets – 2
- Lemon juice – 2 tbsps.
- Salt and black pepper to taste
- Garlic powder – ½ tsp.
- Water – 1/3 cup
- Soy sauce – 1/3 cup
- Scallions – 3, chopped
- Brown sugar – 1/3 cup
- Olive oil – 2 tbsps.

Directions:

In a bowl, mix water, sugar, garlic powder, soy sauce, salt, pepper, oil, and lemon juice. Whisk well and add salmon fillets. Coat well and marinate in the refrigerator for 1 hour. Cook salmon in the air-fryer at 360F for 8 minutes. Flip once. Divide salmon on plates. Sprinkle scallions to the top and serve.

Lemony Saba Fish

Cook time: 8 minutes |Serves: 2| Per serving: Calories 300; Carbs 15g; Fat 4g; Protein 15g

Ingredients:

- Saba fish fillet – 4, boneless
- Salt and black pepper to taste
- Red chili pepper – 3, chopped
- Lemon juice – 2 tbsps.

- o Olive oil – 2 tbsps.
- o Garlic – 2 tbsps. minced

Directions:

Season fish fillets with salt and pepper and place in a bowl. Add garlic, chili, oil, and lemon juice and toss to coat. Transfer fish to the air fryer and cook at 360F for 8 minutes. Flipping halfway. Serve.

Asian Halibut

Cook time: 10 minutes |Serves: 3| Per serving: Calories 286; Carbs 14g; Fat 5g; Protein 23g

Ingredients:

- o Halibut steaks – 1 pound
- o Soy sauce – 2/3 cup
- o Sugar – ¼ cup
- o Lime juice – 2 tbsps.
- o Mirin – ½ cup
- o Red pepper flakes – ¼ tsp. crushed
- o Orange juice – ¼ cup
- o Ginger – ¼ tsp. grated
- o Garlic – 1 clove, minced

Directions:

Pour soy sauce in a pan and heat over medium heat. Add garlic, ginger, pepper flakes, orange juice, lime, sugar, and mirin. Stir well, bring to a boil and take off the heat. Transfer half of the marinade to a bowl, add halibut, toss to coat and marinate in the refrigerator for 30 minutes. Cook halibut in the air fryer at 390F for 10 minutes. Flipping once. Divide halibut steaks on plates, drizzle the rest of the marinade all over and serve.

Shrimp and Crab Mix

Cook time: 25 minutes |Serves: 4| Per serving: Calories 200; Carbs 17g; Fat 13g; Protein 19g

Ingredients:

- o Yellow onion – ½ cup, chopped

- o Green bell pepper – 1 cup, chopped

- o Celery – 1 cup, chopped

- o Shrimp – 1 cup, peeled and deveined

- o Crabmeat – 1 cup, flaked

- o Mayonnaise – 1 cup

- o Worcestershire sauce – 1 tsp.

- o Salt and black pepper to taste

- o Breadcrumbs – 2 tbsps.

- o Butter – 1 tbsp. melted

- o Sweet paprika -1 tsp.

Directions:

In a bowl, mix crab meat, shrimp, onion, bell pepper, celery, mayo, salt, pepper and Worcestershire sauce. Transfer to a pan. Add melted butter, paprika, and bread crumbs. Coat well and place in the air fryer. Cook at 320F for 25 minutes. Shake once at the halfway mark. Serve.

Seafood Casserole
Cook time: 40 minutes |Serves: 6| Per serving: Calories 270; Carbs 15g; Fat 32g; Protein 23g

Ingredients:

- o Butter – 6 tbsps.

- o Mushrooms – 2 ounces, chopped

- o Green bell pepper – 1 small, chopped

- o Celery – 1 stalk, chopped

- o Garlic – 2 cloves, minced

- o Small yellow onion – 1, chopped

- o Salt and black pepper to taste

- o Flour – 4 tbsps.

- o White wine – ½ cup

- o   Milk – 1 ½ cups

- o   Heavy cream – ½ cup

- o   Sea scallops – 4, sliced

- o   Haddock – 4 ounces, skinless, boneless and cut into small pieces

- o   Lobster meat – 4 ounces, cooked and cut into small pieces

- o   Mustard powder – ½ tsp.

- o   Lemon juice – 1 tbsp.

- o   Bread crumbs – 1/3 cup

- o   Salt and black pepper to taste

- o   Cheddar cheese – 3 tbsps. grated

- o   Handful parsley, chopped

- o   Sweet paprika – 1 tsp.

Directions:

Heat 4 tbsps. of butter in a pan over a medium-high heat. Add wine, onion, garlic, celery, mushrooms, and bell pepper and cook for 10 minutes. Add milk, cream, and flour, stir well and cook for 6 minutes. Add haddock, lobster meat, scallops, mustard powder, salt, pepper, and lemon juice and stir well. Remove from heat and place in a pan. In a bowl, mix the rest of the butter with cheese, paprika, and bread crumbs and sprinkle over seafood mix. Transfer the pan to the air fryer and cook at 360F for 16 minutes. Serve garnish with parsley.

Chapter 5 Beef, Lamb and Pork

Rib Eye Steak

Cook time: 20 minutes |Serves: 4| Per serving: Calories 320; Carbs 22g; Fat 8g; Protein 21g

Ingredients:

- o   Ribeye steak – 2 pounds
- o   Salt and black pepper to taste
- o   Olive oil – 1 tbsp.

For the rub

- o   Sweet paprika – 3 tbsps.
- o   Onion powder – 2 tbsps.
- o   Garlic powder – 2 tbsps.
- o   Brown sugar – 1 tbsp.
- o   Oregano – 2 tbsps. dried
- o   Cumin – 1 tbsp. ground
- o   Rosemary – 1 tbsp. dried

Directions:

Mix cumin, salt, pepper, rosemary, oregano, sugar, garlic powder, onion powder and paprika in a bowl. Stir and rub steak with this mix. Season steak with salt, pepper, and rub again with the oil. Place in the air fryer and cook at 400F for 20 minutes. Flipping once. Slice and serve.

Steak and Broccoli

Cook time: 12 minutes |Serves: 4| Per serving: Calories 330; Carbs 23g; Fat 12g; Protein 23g

Ingredients:

- o   Round steak – ¾ pound, cut into strips

- o   Broccoli florets – 1 pound

- o   Oyster sauce – 1/3 cup

- o   Sesame oil – 2 tsps.

- o   Soy sauce – 1 tsp.

- o   Sugar – 1 tsp.

- o   Sherry – 1/3 cup

- o   Olive oil – 1 tbsp.

- o   Garlic – 1 clove, minced

Directions:

In a bowl, mix sugar, sherry, soy sauce, oyster sauce, and sesame oil. Add beef, toss to coat and marinate for 30 minutes. Transfer to a bowl. Add oil, garlic, and broccoli. Toss to coat. Cook at 380F for 12 minutes. Serve.

Provencal Pork

Cook time: 15 minutes |Serves: 2| Per serving: Calories 300; Carbs 21g; Fat 8g; Protein 23g

Ingredients:

- o   Red onion – 1, sliced

- o   Yellow bell pepper – 1, cut into strips

- o   Green bell pepper – 1, cut into strips

- o   Salt and black pepper to taste

- o   Provencal herbs – 2 tsps.

- o   Mustard – ½ tsp.

- o   Olive oil – 1 tbsp.

- o   Pork tenderloin – 7 ounces

Directions:

In a dish, mix salt, pepper, onion, green bell pepper, yellow bell pepper, half the oil, and herbs and toss well. Season pork with mustard, salt, pepper, and rest of the oil. Toss well and add to veggies. Cook in the air fryer at 370F for 15 minutes. Serve.

Lamb and Brussels Sprouts

Cook time: 70 minutes |Serves: 4| Per serving: Calories 440; Carbs 2g; Fat 23g; Protein 49g

Ingredients:

- o   Leg of lamb – 2 pounds, scored
- o   Olive oil – 2 tbsps.
- o   Rosemary - 1 tbsp. chopped
- o   Lemon thyme – 1 tbsp. chopped
- o   Garlic – 1 clove, minced
- o   Brussels sprouts – 1 ½ pounds trimmed
- o   Butter – 1 tbsp. melted
- o   Sour cream – ½ cup
- o   Salt and black pepper to taste

Directions:

Season the leg of lamb with rosemary, thyme, salt, and pepper. Brush with oil, and place in the air fryer basket. Cook at 300F for 1 hour. Flip once at the halfway mark. Transfer to a plate and keep warm. In a pan, mix Brussels sprouts with sour cream, butter, garlic, salt, and pepper. Mix well and cook at 400F for 10 minutes. Divide lamb on plates, add Brussels sprouts on the side and serve.

Beef with Peas and Mushrooms

Cook time: 22 minutes |Serves: 2| Per serving: Calories 235; Carbs 22g; Fat 8g; Protein 24g

Ingredients:

- o   Beef steaks – 2, cut into strips
- o   Salt and black pepper to taste
- o   Snow peas – 7 ounces
- o   White mushrooms – 8 ounces, halved

- o   Yellow onion – 1, cut into rings

- o   Soy sauce – 2 tbsps.

- o   Olive oil – 1 tsp.

Directions:

In a bowl, mix soy sauce, and olive oil, and whisk. Add beef strips and coat. In another bowl, mix mushrooms, onion, snow peas with salt, pepper, and the oil. Toss well. Place in pan and cook in the air fryer at 350F for 16 minutes. Add beef strips to the pan as well and cook at 400F for 6 minutes more. Serve.

Lamb Chops
Cook time: 10 minutes |Serves: 4| Per serving: Calories 231; Carbs 14g; Fat 7g; Protein 23g

Ingredients:

- o   Olive oil – 3 tbsps.

- o   Lamb chops – 8

- o   Salt and black pepper to taste

- o   Garlic – 4 cloves, minced

- o   Oregano – 1 tbsp. chopped

- o   Coriander – 1 tbsp. chopped

Directions:

In a bowl, mix oregano with garlic, oil, salt, pepper, and lamb chops and coat well. Cook in the air fryer at 400F for 10 minutes. Serve.

Crispy Lamb
Cook time: 30 minutes |Serves: 4| Per serving: Calories 230; Carbs 10g; Fat 2g; Protein 12g

Ingredients:

- o   Bread crumbs – 1 tbsp.

- o   Macadamia nuts – 2 tbsps. toasted and crushed

- o   Olive oil – 1 tbsp.

- o   Garlic – 1 clove, minced

- o   Rack of lamb – 28 ounces

- o   Salt and black pepper to taste

- o   Egg – 1

- o   Rosemary – 1 tbsp. chopped

Directions:

Mix oil, and garlic in a bowl and stir well. Season lamb with salt, pepper, and brush with oil. In another bowl, mix nuts with rosemary and breadcrumbs. Put the egg in a separate bowl and whisk well. Dip lamb in egg, then in the macadamia mix, place them in your air fryer's basket. Cook at 360F for 25 minutes. Then increase heat to 400F and cook for 5 minutes more. Serve.

Indian Pork
Cook time: 12 minutes |Serves: 4| Per serving: Calories 423; Carbs 42g; Fat 11g; Protein 18g

Ingredients:

- o   Ginger powder – 1 tsp.

- o   Chili paste – 2 tsps.

- o   Garlic cloves – 2, minced

- o   Pork chops – 14 ounces, cubed

- o   Shallot – 1, chopped

- o   Coriander – 1 tsp. ground

- o   Coconut milk – 7 ounces

- o   Olive oil – 2 tbsps.

- o   Peanuts – 3 ounces, ground

- o   Soy sauce - 3 tbsps.

- o   Salt and black pepper to taste

Directions:

In a bowl, mix ginger with half the oil, half of the soy sauce, half of the garlic, and 1 tsp. chili paste. Whisk and add meat. Coat and marinate for 10 minutes. Cook the meat at 400F in the air fryer for 12 minutes. Meanwhile, heat up the pan with the rest of the oil and add the rest of the peanuts, coconut milk, coriander, rest of the garlic, rest of the chili paste, rest of the soy sauce, and shallot — Stir-Fry for 5 minutes. Divide pork on plates, spread coconut mix on top and serve.

Beef with Mayo

Cook time: 40 minutes |Serves: 8| Per serving: Calories 400; Carbs 27g; Fat 12g; Protein 19g

Ingredients:

- o   Mayonnaise – 1 cup
- o   Sour cream – 1/3 cup
- o   Garlic – 3 cloves, minced
- o   Beef fillet – 3 pounds
- o   Chives – 2 tbsps. chopped
- o   Mustard – 2 tbsps.
- o   Tarragon – ¼ cup, chopped
- o   Salt and black pepper to taste

Directions:

Season beef with salt and pepper and place in the air fryer. Cook at 370F for 20 minutes. Transfer to a plate and set aside. In a bowl, mix garlic with salt, pepper, mayo, chives, and sour cream. Whisk and set aside. In another bowl, mix mustard with tarragon, and Dijon mustard. Whisk, and add beef. Mix well. Return to the air fryer and cook at 350F for 20 minutes more. Divide beef on plates, spread garlic mayo on top and serve.

Marinated Beef

Cook time: 45 minutes |Serves: 6| Per serving: Calories 500; Carbs 29g; Fat 9g; Protein 36g

Ingredients:

- o   Bacon strips – 6
- o   Butter – 2 tbsps.
- o   Garlic – 3 cloves, minced
- o   Salt and black pepper to taste
- o   Horseradish – 1 tbsp.
- o   Mustard – 1 tbsp.
- o   Beef roast – 3 pounds
- o   Beef stock – 1 ¾ cups

- Red wine – ¾ cup

Directions:

In a bowl, mix butter with horseradish, salt, pepper, garlic, and mustard. Whisk and rub the beef with this mix. Arrange bacon strips on a cutting board. Place beef on top and fold bacon around beef. Place in the air fryer basket and cook at 400F for 15 minutes and transfer to a pan. Add stock and wine to the beef. Place the pan in the air fryer and cook at 360F for 30 minutes. Carve beef, divide among plates, and serve.

Creamy Pork

Cook time: 22 minutes |Serves: 6| Per serving: Calories 300; Carbs 26g; Fat 4g; Protein 34g

Ingredients:

  - Pork meat – 2 pounds, boneless and cubed
  - Yellow onions – 2, chopped
  - Olive oil – 1 tbsp.
  - Garlic – 1 clove, minced
  - Chicken stock – 3 cups
  - Sweet paprika – 2 tbsps.
  - Salt and black pepper to taste
  - White flour – 2 tbsps.
  - Sour cream – 1 ½ cups
  - Dill – 2 tbsps. chopped

Directions:

In a pan, mix pork with oil, salt, and pepper. Mix and place in the air fryer. Cook at 360F for 7 minutes. Add the sour cream, dill, flour, paprika, stock, garlic, and onion and mix. Cook at 370F for 15 minutes more. Serve.

Pork Chops with Onions

Cook time: 25 minutes |Serves: 2| Per serving: Calories 384; Carbs 17g; Fat 4g; Protein 25g

Ingredients:

  - Pork chops – 2

- o Olive oil – ¼ cup

- o Yellow onions – 2, sliced

- o Garlic cloves – 2, minced

- o Mustard – 2 tsps.

- o Sweet paprika – 1 tsp.

- o Salt and black pepper to taste

- o Oregano – ½ tsp. dried

- o Thyme – ½ tsp. dried

- o A pinch of cayenne pepper

Directions:

In a bowl, mix oil with cayenne, thyme, oregano, black pepper, paprika, mustard, and garlic. Whisk well. Combine onions with meat and mustard mix. Toss to coat, cover and marinate in the refrigerator for 1 day. Transfer meat and onions mix to a pan and cook in the air fryer at 360F for 25 minutes. Serve.

Braised Pork
Cook time: 40 minutes |Serves: 4| Per serving: Calories 320; Carbs 29g; Fat 4g; Protein 38g

Ingredients:

- o Pork loin roast – 2 pounds, boneless and cubed

- o Butter – 4 tbsps. melted

- o Salt and black pepper to taste

- o Chicken stock – 2 cups

- o Dry white wine – ½ cup

- o Garlic – 2 cloves, minced

- o Thyme – 1 tsp. chopped

- o Thyme spring – 1

- o Bay leaf – 1

- o Yellow onion – ½, chopped

- White flour – 2 tbsps.
- Red grapes – ½ pound

Directions:

Season pork cubes with salt and pepper. Rub with 2 tbsps. melted butter and put in the air fryer. Cook at 370F for 8 minutes. Meanwhile, heat up a pan with 2 tbsps. of butter over a medium heat. Add onion and garlic, and stir-fry for 2 minutes. Add a bay leaf, flour, thyme, salt, pepper, stock, and wine. Mix well. Bring to a simmer and take off the heat. Add grapes and pork cubes. Cook in the air fryer at 360F for 30 minutes. Serve.

Pork with Couscous
Cook time: 35 minutes |Serves: 6| Per serving: Calories 310; Carbs 37g; Fat 4g; Protein 34g

Ingredients:

- Pork loin – 2 ½ pounds, boneless, and trimmed
- Chicken stock – ¾ cup
- Olive oil – 2 tbsps.
- Sweet paprika – ½ tbsp.
- Dried sage – 2 ¼ tsps.
- Garlic powder – ½ tsp.
- Dried rosemary – ¼ tsp.
- Dried marjoram – ¼ tsp.
- Dried basil – 1 tsp.
- Dried oregano – 1 tsp.
- Salt and black pepper to taste
- Couscous – 2 cups, cooked

Directions:

In a bowl, mix oil with stock, salt, pepper, oregano, marjoram, thyme, rosemary, sage, garlic powder, and paprika. Whisk well and add pork loin. Mix and marinate for 1 hour. Cook in the air fryer at 370F for 35 minutes. Divide among plates and serve with couscous on the side.

Beef and Green Onions

Cook time: 20 minutes |Serves: 4| Per serving: Calories 329; Carbs 26g; Fat 8g; Protein 22g

Ingredients:

- Green onion - 1 cup, chopped
- Soy sauce – 1 cup
- Water – ½ cup
- Brown sugar – ¼ cup
- Sesame seeds – ¼ cup
- Garlic – 5 cloves, minced
- Black pepper – 1 tsp.
- Lean beef – 1 pound

Directions:

In a bowl, mix the onion with water, soy sauce, garlic, sugar, sesame seeds, and pepper. Whisk and add meat. Marinate for 10 minutes. Drain beef. Cook in the preheated 390F air fryer for 20 minutes. Serve.

Lamb with Veggies

Cook time: 30 minutes |Serves: 4| Per serving: Calories 265; Carbs 18g; Fat 3g; Protein 22g

Ingredients:

- Carrot – 1, chopped
- Onion – 1, sliced
- Olive oil – ½ tbsp.
- Bean sprouts – 3 ounces
- Lamb loin – 8 ounces, sliced

For the marinade

- Garlic – 1 clove, minced
- Apple – ½, grated
- Salt and black pepper to taste

- ○ Small yellow onion – 1, grated

- ○ Grated ginger – 1 tbsp.

- ○ Soy sauce – 5 tbsps.

- ○ Sugar – 1 tbsp.

- ○ Orange juice – 2 tbsps.

Directions:

In a bowl, mix 1 grated onion with black pepper, sugar, orange juice, soy sauce, 1 tbsp. ginger, garlic, and apple. Whisk and add the lamb. Coat and marinate for 10 minutes. Heat olive oil in a pan over a medium-high heat. Add 1 sliced onion, bean sprouts, and carrot. Stir-Fry for 3 minutes. Add lamb and the marinade. Place the pan in the preheat air fryer and cook at 360F for 25 minutes. Serve.

Creamy Lamb

Cook time: 1 hour |Serves: 8| Per serving: Calories 287; Carbs 19g; Fat 4g; Protein 25g

Ingredients:

- ○ Leg of lamb – 5 pounds

- ○ Buttermilk – 2 cups

- ○ Mustard – 2 tbsps.

- ○ Butter – ½ cup

- ○ Basil – 2 tbsps. chopped

- ○ Tomato paste – 2 tbsps.

- ○ Garlic – 2 cloves, minced

- ○ Salt and black pepper to taste

- ○ White wine – 1 cup

- ○ Cornstarch – 1 tbsp. mixed with 1 tbsp. water

- ○ Sour cream – ½ cup

Directions:

Place lamb roast in a dish. Add buttermilk and toss to coat. Cover and marinate in the refrigerator for 24 hours. Pat dry lamb and put in a pan that fits in the air fryer basket. In a bowl, mix butter with garlic, salt, pepper, rosemary, basil, mustard, and tomato paste. Whisk well and spread over the lamb. Place in the air fryer and cook at 300F for 1 hour. Slice lamb, divide among plates. Heat up cooking juices from the pan on the stove. Add sour cream, salt, pepper, wine, and cornstarch mix. Remove from heat and drizzle lamb with this sauce. Serve.

Lamb Shanks

Cook time: 45 minutes |Serves: 4| Per serving: Calories 283; Carbs 17g; Fat 4g; Protein 26g

Ingredients:

- o   Lamb shanks – 4
- o   Yellow onion – 1, chopped
- o   Olive oil – 1 tbsp.
- o   Coriander seeds – 4 tsps. crushed
- o   White flour – 2 tbsps.
- o   Bay leaves – 4
- o   Honey – 2 tsps.
- o   Dry sherry – 5 ounces
- o   Chicken stock – 2 ½ cups
- o   Salt and pepper to taste

Directions:

Season the lamb shanks with salt and pepper. Rub with half of the oil and cook in the air fryer at 360F for 10 minutes. Heat up a pan that fits in the air fryer with the rest of the oil over medium-high heat. Add onion and coriander. Stir and cook for 5 minutes. Add salt, pepper, bay leaves, honey, stock, sherry, and flour. Stir, bring to a simmer, and add the lamb. Mix well. Cook in the air fryer at 360F for 30 minutes. Serve.

Lamb with Potatoes

Cook time: 45 minutes |Serves: 6| Per serving: Calories 273; Carbs 25g; Fat 4g; Protein 29g

Ingredients:

- o   Lamb roast – 4 pounds
- o   Rosemary – 1 spring

- o   Garlic – 3 cloves, minced

- o   Potatoes – 6, halved

- o   Lamb stock – ½ cup

- o   Bay leaves – 4

- o   Salt and pepper to taste

Directions:

Put potatoes in a dish. Add salt, pepper, rosemary spring, garlic, bay leaves, stock, and lamb. Mix and place in the air fryer. Cook at 360F for 45 minutes. Slice lamb, divide among plates, and serve with potatoes and cooking juices.

Classic Mini Meatloaf
Cook time: 25 minutes |Serves: 6| Per serving: Calories 170; Carbs 2.6g; Fat 9.4g; Protein 14.9g

Ingredients:

- o   80/20 ground beef – 1 pound

- o   Yellow onion – ¼, diced

- o   Green bell pepper – ½, diced

- o   Egg – 1

- o   Almond flour – 3 tbsps.

- o   Worcestershire sauce – 1 tbsp.

- o   Garlic powder – ½ tsp.

- o   Dried parsley – 1 tsp.

- o   Tomato paste – 2 tbsps.

- o   Water – ¼ cup

- o   Powdered brown sugar – 1 tbsp.

Directions:

In a bowl, combine almond flour, egg, pepper, onion, and ground beef. Pour in Worcestershire sauce and add the parsley and garlic powder to the bowl. Mix well. Divide the mixture into two and place into two loaf baking pans. In another bowl, mix the sugar, water, and tomato paste. Spoon half the mixture over each loaf. Place loaf pans into the air fryer basket, working in batches. Cook at 350F for 25 minutes. Serve warm.

Chorizo and Beef Burger

Cook time: 15 minutes |Serves: 4| Per serving: Calories 291; Carbs 3.8g; Fat 18.3g; Protein 21.6g

Ingredients:

- 80/20 ground beef – ¾ pound
- Ground chorizo – ¼ pound
- Chopped onion – ¼ cup
- Pickled jalapenos – 5 slices, chopped
- Chili powder – 2 tsps.
- Minced garlic -1 tsp.
- Cumin – ¼ tsp.

Directions:

Mix all the ingredients in a bowl. Make four burger patties from the mixture. Place burger patties into the air fryer basket. Cook at 375F for 15 minutes. Flip once. Serve.

Stuffed Peppers

Cook time: 30 minutes |Serves: 4| Per serving: Calories 346; Carbs 7.2g; Fat 19.1g; Protein 27.8g

Ingredients:

- 80/20 ground beef – 1 pound
- Chili powder – 1 tbsp.
- Cumin – 2 tsps.
- Garlic powder – 1 tsp.
- Salt – 1 tsp.
- Ground black pepper – ¼ tsp.
- Diced tomatoes and green chilies – 1 (10-ounce) can, drained
- Green bell peppers – 4, cut in half (seeds and membrane removed)
- Shredded Monterey jack cheese – 1 cup, divided

Directions:

Brown the ground beef in the Instant Pot for 7 to 10 minutes on Sauté. Then drain the fat. Add cumin, chili powder, salt, black pepper, and garlic powder. Add drained tomatoes and chilies. Cook for 3 to 5 minutes. Spoon the cooked mixture evenly into bell pepper halves and top with ¼-cup cheese. Place the stuffed peppers into the air fryer basket. Cook at 350F for 15 minutes. Serve.

Italian Stuffed Bell Peppers
Cook time: 25 minutes |Serves: 4| Per serving: Calories 358; Carbs 8.7g; Fat 24.1g; Protein 21.1g

Ingredients:

- o   Ground pork Italian sausage – 1 pound
- o   Garlic powder – ½ tsp.
- o   Dried parsley – ½ tsp.
- o   Diced Roma tomato – 1
- o   Chopped onion – ¼ cup
- o   Green bell pepper – 4
- o   Shredded mozzarella cheese – 1 cup, divided

Directions:

Brown the ground sausage on Sauté in the Instant Pot until no longer pink. Drain fat. Add the onion, tomato, parsley, and garlic powder. Cook for 3 to 5 minutes more. Slice peppers in half and remove the seeds and white membrane. Spoon the meat mixture evenly into pepper halves. Top with mozzarella and place pepper halves into the air fryer basket. Cook at 350F for 15 minutes. Serve.

Bacon Casserole
Cook time: 20 minutes |Serves: 4| Per serving: Calories 369; Carbs 1g; Fat 22.6g; Protein 31g

Ingredients:

- o   80/20 ground beef – 1 pound
- o   White onion – ¼, chopped
- o   Shredded cheddar cheese – 1 cup, divided
- o   Egg – 1
- o   Bacon – 4 slices, cooked and crumbled

- o   Pickle spears – 2, chopped

Directions:

Brown the ground beef in the Instant Pot on Sauté for 7 to 10 minutes. Drain the fat. Add the ground beef to a bowl. Add egg, ½-cup cheddar and onion to the bowl. Mix well and add crumbled bacon. Pour the mixture into a round baking dish and top with remaining cheddar. Place into the air fryer basket. Cook at 375F for 20 minutes. Serve topped with chopped pickles.

Spicy Lamb Sirloin Steak
Cook time: 15 minutes |Serves: 4| Per serving: Calories 171; Carbs 4g; Fat 22.1g; Protein 24g

Ingredients:

- o   Onion – ½, chopped

- o   Ginger – 4 cubes, chopped

- o   Garlic – 5 cloves, chopped

- o   Garam masala – 1 tsp.

- o   Fennel – 1 tsp. ground

- o   Cinnamon – 1 tsp. ground

- o   Cayenne powder – ½ tsp.

- o   Salt – 1 tsp.

- o   Lamb sirloin – 1-pound, boneless

Directions:

Add all the ingredients in a blender except for the lamb chops and blend until paste. Make strips over the lamb chops. Rub the paste on the chops and mix well. Marinate overnight. Grease the air fryer basket. Place the lamb steaks in the air fryer grease with cooking spray. Bake at 380F for 15 minutes. Flip the meat at the halfway mark. Serve.

Herb Rack of Lamb
Cook time: 20 minutes |Serves: 2| Per serving: Calories 414; Carbs 3g; Fat 46.7g; Protein 47g

Ingredients:

- o   Whole rack of lamb – 1 pound

- o   Rosemary – 2 tbsps. dried

- o   Thyme – 1 tbsp. dried

- o   Garlic – 2 tsps. minced

- o   Salt and pepper to taste

- o   Olive oil – 4 tbsps.

Directions:

In a bowl, mix everything except for the lamb. Rub the lamb with the herb mixture and coat well. Cook in the air fryer at 360F for 10 minutes. Flip once at the halfway mark. Serve.

Pulled Pork

Cook time: 2 ½ hours |Serves: 8| Per serving: Calories 537; Carbs 0.7g; Fat 35.5g; Protein 42.6g

Ingredients:

- o   Chili powder – 2 tbsps.

- o   Garlic powder – 1 tsp.

- o   Onion powder – ½ tsp.

- o   Ground black pepper – ½ tsp.

- o   Cumin – ½ tsp.

- o   Pork shoulder – 1 (4-pound)

Directions:

In a bowl, mix cumin, pepper, onion powder, garlic powder, and chili powder. Rub the spice mixture over the pork shoulder, patting it into the skin. Place the pork shoulder into the air fryer basket. Cook at 350F for 150 minutes. Shred the meat with forks and serve.

Baby Back Ribs

Cook time: 25 minutes |Serves: 4| Per serving: Calories 650; Carbs 2.8g; Fat 51.5g; Protein 40.4g

Ingredients:

- o   Baby back ribs – 2 pounds

- o   Chili powder – 2 tsps.

- o   Paprika – 1 tsp.

- o   Onion powder – ½ tsp.

- o   Garlic powder – ½ tsp.

- o   Ground cayenne pepper – ¼ tsp.

- o   Barbecue sauce – ½ cup

Directions:

Except for the barbecue sauce, rub ribs with the rest of the ingredients. Place into the air fryer basket. Cook at 400F for 25 minutes. Flip once. Brush ribs with barbecue sauce and serve.

Juicy Pork Chops
Cook time: 15 minutes |Serves: 2 | Per serving: Calories 313; Carbs 1.1g; Fat 22.6g; Protein 24.4g

Ingredients:

- o   Chili powder – 1 tsp.

- o   Garlic powder – ½ tsp.

- o   Cumin – ½ tsp.

- o   Ground black pepper – ¼ tsp.

- o   Dried oregano – ¼ tsp.

- o   Boneless pork chops – 2 (4-ounce)

- o   Unsalted butter – 2 tbsps. divided

Directions:

Mix oregano, pepper, cumin, garlic powder, and chili powder in a bowl. Rub dry rub onto pork chops. Place pork chops into the air fryer basket. Cook at 400F for 15 minutes. Serve each chop topped with 1 tbsp. butter.

Reverse Seared Ribeye
Cook time: 45 minutes |Serves: 2| Per serving: Calories 377; Carbs 0.4g; Fat 30.7g; Protein 22.6g

Ingredients:

- o   Ribeye steak – 1 (8-ounce)

- o   Salt – ½ tsp.

- o Ground peppercorn – ¼ tsp.

- o Coconut oil – 1 tbsp.

- o Salted butter – 1 tbsp. softened

- o Garlic powder – ¼ tsp.

- o Dried parsley – ½ tsp.

- o Dried oregano – ¼ tsp.

Directions:

Rub steak with salt and ground peppercorn. Place into the air fryer basket. Cook at 250F for 45 minutes. Check for doneness and cook a few minutes more if necessary. Remove the steak. Heat coconut oil in the Instant Pot on Sauté. Sear the steak until crisp and browned. Remove from heat and allow to rest. Whip butter with oregano, parsley, and garlic powder in a bowl. Slice steak and serve with herb butter on top.

Beef and Broccoli Stir-Fry
Cook time: 20 minutes |Serves: 2| Per serving: Calories 342; Carbs 6.9g; Fat 18.9g; Protein 27g

Ingredients:

- o Sirloin steak – ½ pound, thinly sliced

- o Liquid aminos – 2 tbsps.

- o Grated ginger – ¼ tsp.

- o Finely minced garlic – ¼ tsp.

- o Coconut oil – 1 tbsp.

- o Broccoli florets – 2 cups

- o Crushed red pepper – ¼ tsp.

- o Xanthan gum – 1/8 tsp.

- o Sesame seeds – ½ tsp.

Directions:

In a bowl, add coconut oil, garlic, ginger, liquid aminos, and beef. Cover and marinate 1 hour in the refrigerator. Remove beef from the marinade, reserving marinade, and place the beef into the air fryer basket. Cook at 320F for 20 minutes. After 10 minutes, add broccoli and sprinkle red pepper into the air fryer basket and shake. Bring the marinade to a boil in a skillet, then reduce heat to simmer. Stir in xanthan gum and allow to thicken. When cooking is done, add the beef and broccoli from the air fryer to the skillet and toss. Sprinkle with sesame seeds and serve.

BBQ Meatballs

Cook time: 14 minutes |Serves: 4| Per serving: Calories 336; Carbs 4g; Fat 19.5g; Protein 28.1g

Ingredients:

- 80/20 ground beef – 1 pound
- Ground Italian sausage – ¼ pound
- Egg – 1
- Onion powder – ¼ tsp.
- Garlic powder – ½ tsp.
- Dried parsley - 1 tsp.
- Bacon – 4 slices, cooked and chopped
- Chopped white onion – ¼ cup
- Chopped pickled jalapenos – ¼ cup
- Barbecue sauce – ½ cup

Directions:

Mix ground beef, sausage and egg in a bowl until fully combined. Mix in all remaining ingredients except barbecue sauce. Make 8 meatballs. Place meatballs into the air fryer basket. Cook at 400F for 14 minutes. Turn once. Remove meatballs from the fryer and toss in barbecue sauce. Serve.

Pork Salad

Cook time: 8 minutes |Serves: 2| Per serving: Calories 526; Carbs 5.2g; Fat 37g; Protein 34.4g

Ingredients:

- Coconut oil – 1 tbsp.
- Pork chops – 2 (4-ounce) chopped into 1-inch cubes
- Chili powder – 2 tsps.
- Paprika – 1 tsp.

- Garlic powder – ½ tsp.

- Onion powder – ¼ tsp.

- Chopped romaine – 4 cups

- Roma tomato – 1 medium, diced

- Shredded Monterey jack cheese – ½ cup

- Avocado – 1, diced

- Full-fat ranch dressing – ¼ cup

- Chopped cilantro – 1 tbsp.

Directions:

Drizzle coconut oil over the pork and sprinkle with onion powder, garlic powder, paprika, and chili powder. Place pork into the air fryer basket. Cook at 400F for 8 minutes. In a bowl, place crispy pork, tomato, and romaine. Top with shredded cheese and avocado. Pour ranch dressing around the bowl and toss to coat. Top with cilantro. Serve.

Meatloaf

Cook time: 25 minutes |Serves: 4| Per serving: Calories 297; Carbs 5.9g; Fat 18.8g; Protein 24.8g

Ingredients:

- Lean beef – 1 pound

- Egg – 1, beaten

- Breadcrumbs – 3 tbsps.

- Onion – 1, chopped

- Fresh thyme – 1 tbsp. chopped

- Salt and pepper to taste

- Mushrooms – 2, sliced

- Olive oil -1 tbsp.

Directions:

Combine egg, beef, breadcrumbs, salt, thyme, onion, and pepper in a bowl. Mix well. Place the mixture to a baking pan and mix in the mushrooms. Coat this mix with oil and cook in the air fryer at 380F for 25 minutes. Cool, slice and serve.

Pork Chops

Cook time: 20 minutes |Serves: 4| Per serving: Calories 400; Carbs 3g; Fat 22.9g; Protein 43g

Ingredients:

- Boneless pork chops – 4
- Shredded parmesan cheese – 7 tbsps.
- Salt and pepper to taste
- Paprika – 1 tsp.
- Garlic powder – 1 tsp.
- Onion powder – 1 tsp.
- Oil – 2 tbsps.

Directions:

Coat the meat with oil. Combine the Parmesan with all the spices. Rub the meat with this mixture. Cook in the air fryer at 380F for 20 minutes. Flip at the halfway mark. Serve.

Chapter 6 Snacks and Appetizers

Coconut Chicken Bites
Cook time: 13 minutes |Serves: 4| Per serving: Calories 252; Carbs 14g; Fat 4g; Protein 24g

Ingredients:

- Garlic powder – 2 tsps.

- Eggs – 2

- Salt and black pepper to taste

- Panko bread crumbs – ¾ cup

- Coconut – ¾ cup, shredded

- Cooking spray

- Chicken tenders – 8

Directions:

Mix eggs with garlic powder, salt, and pepper in a bowl and whisk well. In another bowl, mix coconut with panko and stir well. Dip chicken tenders in the eggs mix and then coat in coconut thoroughly. Spray chicken bits with cooking spray. Place them in the air fryer basket and cook them at 350F for 10 minutes. Serve.

Buffalo Cauliflower Snack
Cook time: 15 minutes |Serves: 4| Per serving: Calories 241; Carbs 8g; Fat 4g; Protein 4g

Ingredients:

- ○ Cauliflower florets – 4 cups

- ○ Panko bread crumbs – 1 cup

- ○ Butter – ¼ cup, melted

- ○ Buffalo sauce – ¼ cup

- ○ Mayonnaise for serving

Directions:

In a bowl, mix butter and buffalo sauce and whisk well. Dip cauliflower florets in the mix and coat them in panko bread crumbs. Place them in the air fryer's basket and cook at 350F for 15 minutes. Serve.

Banana Snack
Cook time: 5 minutes |Serves: 2| Per serving: Calories 70; Carbs 10g; Fat 4g; Protein 1g

Ingredients:

- ○ Peanut butter – ¼ cup

- ○ Chocolate chips – ¾ cup

- ○ Banana – 1, peeled and sliced in 16 pieces

- ○ Vegetable oil – 1 tbsp.

Other

- ○ 16 baking cups crust

Directions:

Melt the chocolate chips in a small pot over a low heat or in the microwave. In a bowl, mix coconut oil with peanut butter and whisk well. Spoon 1 tsp. chocolate mix in a cup, add 1 banana sliced and top with 1 tsp. butter mix. Repeat with the rest of the cups; place them all into a dish that fits the air fryer. Cook at 320F for 5 minutes. Cool, freeze and serve.

Apple Snack
Cook time: 5 minutes |Serves: 4| Per serving: Calories 200; Carbs 20g; Fat 4g; Protein 3g

Ingredients:

- ○ Big apples – 3, cored, peeled and cubed

- ○ Lemon juice – 2 tsps.

- o   Pecans – ¼ cup, chopped

- o   Dark chocolate chips – ½ cup

- o   Clean caramel sauce – ½ cup

Directions:

Mix apples and lemon juice in a bowl. Add to a dish that fits in the air fryer. Add pecans, chocolate chips, and drizzle the caramel sauce. Toss to coat. Cook at 320F for 5 minutes in the air fryer. Serve.

Shrimp Muffins

Cook time: 26 minutes |Serves: 6 | Per serving: Calories 160; Carbs 14g; Fat 6g; Protein 4g

Ingredients:

- o   Spaghetti squash – 1, peeled and halved

- o   Mayonnaise – 2 tbsps.

- o   Mozzarella – 1 cup, shredded

- o   Shrimp – 8 ounces, peeled, cooked, and chopped

- o   Panko – 1 ½ cups

- o   Parsley flakes – 1 tsp.

- o   Garlic clove – 1, minced

- o   Salt and black pepper to taste

- o   Cooking spray

Directions:

Place squash halves in the air fryer. Cook at 350F for 16 minutes. Cool and scrape flesh into a bowl. Add mozzarella, mayo, shrimp, panko, parsley flakes, pepper, and salt. Mix well. Spray a muffin tray with cooking spray and divide squash and shrimp mix in each cup. Place in the air fryer and cook at 360F for 10 minutes. Serve.

Zucchini Cakes

Cook time: 12 minutes |Serves: 12| Per serving: Calories 60; Carbs 6g; Fat 1g; Protein 2g

Ingredients:

- o   Cooking spray

- o Dill – ½ cup, chopped

- o Egg – 1

- o Whole wheat flour – ½ cup

- o Salt and black pepper to taste

- o Yellow onion – 1, chopped

- o Garlic cloves – 2, minced

- o Zucchinis – 3, grated

Directions:

In a bowl, mix zucchinis with dill, egg, salt, pepper, flour, onion, and garlic. Mix thoroughly. Make small patties with the mix and spray them with cooking spray. Place them in the air fryer basket and cook at 370F for 6 minutes on each side. Serve.

Pesto Crackers

Cook time: 17 minutes |Serves: 6| Per serving: Calories 200; Carbs 4g; Fat 20g; Protein 7g

Ingredients:

- o Baking powder – ½ tsp.

- o Salt and black pepper to taste

- o Flour – 1 ¼ cups

- o Basil – ¼ tsp. dried

- o Garlic – 1 clove, minced

- o Basil pesto - 2 tbsps.

- o Butter – 3 tbsps.

Directions:

Mix butter, pesto, basil, cayenne, garlic, flour, baking powder, salt, and pepper in a bowl and make a dough. Spread the dough on a lined baking sheet. Bake in the air fryer at 325F for 17 minutes. Cool and cut into crackers. Serve.

Pumpkin Muffins

Cook time: 15 minutes |Serves: 18| Per serving: Calories 50; Carbs 2g; Fat 3g; Protein 2g

Ingredients:

- o   Butter – ¼ cup
- o   Pumpkin puree – ¾ cup
- o   Flaxseed meal – 2 tbsps.
- o   Flour – ¼ cup
- o   Sugar – ½ cup
- o   Nutmeg – ½ tsp. ground
- o   Cinnamon powder – 1 tsp.
- o   Baking powder – ½ tsp.
- o   Egg – 1
- o   Baking powder – ½ tsp.

Directions:

Mix butter, pumpkin puree and egg in a bowl and blend well. Add cinnamon, nutmeg, baking powder, baking soda, sugar, flour and flaxseed meal. Spoon this into a muffin pan. Bake in the air-fryer at 350F for 15 minutes. Serve.

Zucchini Chips
Cook time: 1 hour |Serves: 6| Per serving: Calories 40; Carbs 3g; Fat 3g; Protein 7g

Ingredients:

- o   Zucchinis – 3, thinly sliced
- o   Salt and black pepper to taste
- o   Olive oil – 2 tbsps.
- o   Balsamic vinegar – 2 tbsps.

Directions:

Mix vinegar, oil, salt, and pepper and whisk well. Add zucchini slices and toss to coat. Cook in the air fryer at 200F for 1 hour. Shake once. Serve.

Beef Jerky

Cook time: 1 hour 30 minutes |Serves: 6| Per serving: Calories 300; Carbs 3g; Fat 12g; Protein 8g

Ingredients:

- Soy sauce – 2 cups
- Worcestershire sauce – ½ cup
- Black peppercorns – 2 tbsps.
- Black pepper – 2 tbsps.
- Beef round – 2 pounds, sliced

Directions:

In a bowl, mix Worcestershire sauce, black pepper, black peppercorns, and soy sauce and whisk well. Add beef slices. Coat and keep in the refrigerator for 6 hours to marinate. Cook in the air-fryer at 370F for 1 hour and 30 minutes. Transfer to a bowl and serve.

Salmon Patties

Cook time: 22 minutes |Serves: 4| Per serving: Calories 231; Carbs 14g; Fat 3g; Protein 4g

Ingredients:

- Big potatoes – 3, boiled, drained and mashed
- Big salmon fillet – 1, skinless, boneless
- Parsley – 2 tbsps. chopped
- Dill – 2 tbsps. chopped
- Salt and black pepper to taste
- Egg – 1
- Bread crumbs – 2 tbsps.
- Cooking spray

Directions:

Place salmon in the air fryer basket and cook at 360F for 10 minutes. Transfer salmon to a cutting board. Cool, flake it and put it in a bowl. Add bread crumbs, egg, parsley, dill, salt, pepper, and mashed potatoes. Mix and shape 8 patties. Place salmon patties in the air fryer basket and spray with cooking oil. Cook at 360F for 12 minutes. Flip once at the halfway mark. Serve.

Banana Chips

Cook time: 15 minutes |Serves: 4| Per serving: Calories 121; Carbs 3g; Fat 1g; Protein 3g

Ingredients:

- o Bananas – 4, peeled and sliced
- o Salt – 1 pinch
- o Turmeric powder – ½ tsp.
- o Chaat masala – ½ tsp.
- o Olive oil – 1 tsp.

Directions:

In a bowl, mix banana slices with oil, chaat masala, turmeric, and salt. Toss and set aside for 10 minutes. Cook in the air fryer at 360F for 15 minutes. Flipping them once. Serve.

Spring Rolls

Cook time: 25 minutes |Serves:2 | Per serving: Calories 214; Carbs 12g; Fat 4g; Protein 4g

Ingredients:

- o Green cabbage – 2 cups, shredded
- o Yellow onions – 2, chopped
- o Carrot – 1 grated
- o Chili pepper – ½, minced
- o Ginger – 1 tbsp.
- o Garlic – 3 cloves, minced
- o Sugar – 1 tsp.
- o Salt and black pepper to taste
- o Soy sauce – 1 tsp.
- o Olive oil – 2 tbsps.
- o Spring roll sheets – 10
- o Corn flour – 2 tbsps.

o Water – 2 tbsps.

Directions:

Heat oil in the Instant Pot pan on Sauté. Add soy sauce, pepper, salt, sugar, garlic, ginger, chili pepper, carrots, onions, and cabbage. Stir-fry for 2 to 3 minutes. Remove and cool down. Cut spring roll sheets in squares, divide cabbage mix on each and roll them. In a bowl, mix cornflour with water, stir well and seal spring rolls with this mix. Place spring rolls in the air fryer basket and cook at 360F for 10 minutes. Flip rolls and cook them for 10 minutes more. Serve.

Crab Sticks
Cook time: 12 minutes |Serves: 4| Per serving: Calories 110; Carbs 4g; Fat 0g; Protein 2g

Ingredients:

o Crabsticks – 10, halved

o Sesame oil – 2 tsps.

o Cajun seasoning – 2 tsps.

Directions:

Put crab sticks in a bowl. Add seasoning and sesame oil. Toss and place in the air fryer basket. Cook at 350F for 12 minutes. Serve.

Chickpeas Snack
Cook time: 10 minutes |Serves: 4| Per serving: Calories 140; Carbs 20g; Fat 1g; Protein 6g

Ingredients:

o Canned chickpeas – 15 ounces, drained

o Cumin – ½ tsp. ground

o Olive oil – 1 tbsp.

o Smoked paprika – 1 tsp.

o Salt and black pepper to taste

Directions:

In a bowl, mix chickpeas with oil, salt, pepper, paprika, and cumin. Toss to coat and place in the air fryer basket. Cook at 390F for 10 minutes. Serve.

Prosciutto-Parmesan Asparagus

Cook time: 10 minutes |Serves: 4| Per serving: Calories 263; Carbs 4.3g; Fat 20.2g; Protein 13.9g

Ingredients:

- o Asparagus – 1 pound
- o Prosciutto – 12 (0.5 ounce) slices
- o Coconut oil – 1 tbsp. melted
- o Lemon juice – 2 tsps.
- o Red pepper flakes – 1/8 tsp.
- o Grated Parmesan cheese – 1/3 cup
- o Salted butter – 2 tbsps. melted

Directions:

On a clean work surface, place a few asparagus spears onto a sliced of prosciutto. Drizzle with lemon juice and coconut oil. Sprinkle Parmesan and red pepper flakes across asparagus. Roll prosciutto around asparagus spears. Place into the air fryer basket. Repeat. Cook at 375F and 10 minutes. Drizzle the asparagus rolls with butter before serving.

Bacon-Wrapped Jalapeno Poppers

Cook time: 12 minutes |Serves: 4| Per serving: Calories 246; Carbs 2g; Fat 17.9g; Protein 14.4g

Ingredients:

- o Jalapenos – 6, membrane and seeds removed (about 4" long each)
- o Full-fat cream cheese – 3 ounces
- o Shredded medium cheddar cheese – 1/3 cup
- o Garlic powder – ¼ tsp.
- o Bacon – 12 slices

Directions:

Place cream cheese, cheddar, and garlic powder in a bowl. Microwave for 30 seconds and stir. Spoon cheese mixture into hollow jalapenos. Wrap a slice of bacon around each jalapeno half, completely covering pepper. Place into the air fryer basket. Cook at 400F for 12 minutes. Flip once. Serve.

Garlic Parmesan Chicken Wings

Cook time: 25 minutes |Serves: 4| Per serving: Calories 356; Carbs 2.1g; Fat 42.1g; Protein 41.8g

Ingredients:

o   Raw chicken wings – 2 pounds

o   Salt – 1 tsp.

o   Garlic powder – ½ tsp.

o   Baking powder – 1 tbsp.

o   Unsalted butter – 4 tbsps. melted

o   Grated Parmesan cheese – 1/3 cup

o   Dried parsley – ¼ tsp.

Directions:

Place chicken wings, salt, ½ tsp. garlic powder, and baking powder in a bowl. Coat and place wings into the air fryer basket. Cook at 400F for 25 minutes. Toss the basket two or 3 times during the cooking time. Combine butter, parmesan, and parsley in a bowl. Remove wings from the air fryer and place into a bowl. Pour the butter mixture over the wings and toss to coat. Serve warm.

Buffalo Chicken Dip

Cook time: 10 minutes |Serves: 4| Per serving: Calories 472; Carbs 6g; Fat 32g; Protein 25g

Ingredients:

o   Cooked chicken breast – 1 cup, diced

o   Full-fat cream cheese – 8 ounces, softened

o   Buffalo sauce – ½ cup

o   Full-fat ranch dressing – 1/3 cup

o   Chopped pickled jalapenos – 1/3 cup

o   Shred cheddar cheese – 1 ½ cups, divided

o   Scallions – 2, sliced

Directions:

Place chicken into a large bowl. Add buffalo sauce, cream cheese, and ranch dressing. Stir to mix well. Fold in jalapenos and 1-cup cheddar. Pour the mixture into a round baking dish and place remaining cheddar on top. Place dish into the air fryer basket. Cook at 350F for 10 minutes. Top with sliced scallions and serve warm.

Cheese Bread

Cook time: 15 minutes |Serves: 4| Per serving: Calories 273; Carbs 2g; Fat 18g; Protein 20g

Ingredients:

- ○ Shredded mozzarella cheese – 2 cups
- ○ Grated parmesan cheese – ¼ cup
- ○ Chopped pickled jalapenos – ¼ cup
- ○ Eggs – 2
- ○ Bacon – 4 slices, cooked and chopped

Directions:

Mix all ingredients in a bowl. Cover the air fryer basket with parchment paper. Press out the mixture into a circle with damp hands. Or you can make two smaller circles. Place the cheese bread into the air fryer basket. Cook at 320F for 15 minutes. Flip the bread with 5 minutes remaining. The bread should be golden brown when fully cooked. Serve warm.

Cheeseburger Dip

Cook time: 10 minutes |Serves: 6| Per serving: Calories 457; Carbs 3.6g; Fat 35g; Protein 21.6g

Ingredients:

- ○ Full-fat cream cheese – 8 ounces
- ○ Full-fat mayonnaise – ¼ cup
- ○ Full-fat sour cream – ¼ cup
- ○ Chopped onion – ¼ cup
- ○ Garlic powder – 1 tsp.
- ○ Worcestershire sauce -1 tbsp.
- ○ Shredded cheddar cheese – 1 ¼ cups, divided
- ○ Cooked 80/20 ground beef – ½ pound
- ○ Bacon – 6 slices, cooked and crumbled

o   Large pickle spears – 2, chopped

Directions:

Place cream cheese in a bowl, and microwave for 45 seconds.   Stir in sour cream, mayonnaise, onion, garlic powder, 1-cup cheddar, and Worcestershire sauce. Add cooked bacon and ground beef. Sprinkle remaining cheddar on top. Place in a bowl and put into the air fryer basket. Cook at 400F for 10 minutes. The dip is done when the top is golden and bubbling. Sprinkle pickles over the dish. Serve warm.

Pork Rind Tortillas
Cook time: 5 minutes |Serves: 4| Per serving: Calories 145; Carbs 1g; Fat 10g; Protein 10.7g

Ingredients:

o   Pork rinds – 1 ounce, ground

o   Shredded mozzarella cheese – ¾ cup

o   Full-fat cream cheese – 2 tbsps. chopped

o   Egg – 1

Directions:

Place mozzarella into a bowl. Add cream cheese then to the bowl. Microwave for 30 seconds, or until both types of cheese are melted. Add the egg and ground pork rinds to the cheese mixture. Stir and make a ball. Separate the dough into four small balls. Place each ball of dough between two sheets of parchment and roll into a ¼ flat layer. Place tortillas into the air fryer basket in a single layer. Set the temperature to 400F and cook for 5 minutes. Serve.

Mozzarella Sticks
Cook time: 10 minutes |Serves: 3| Per serving: Calories 236; Carbs 4.7g; Fat 13.8g; Protein 19.2g

Ingredients:

o   Mozzarella string cheese sticks – 6 (1-ounce)

o   Grated Parmesan cheese – ½ cup

o   Pork rinds – ½ ounce, finely ground

o   Dried parsley – 1 tsp.

o   Eggs – 2

Directions:

Cut the mozzarella sticks in half. Freeze until firm. In a bowl, mix ground pork rinds, Parmesan, and parsley. Whisk eggs in another bowl. Dip a frozen mozzarella stick into beaten eggs and then into the Parmesan mixture to coat. Repeat with the remaining sticks. Place mozzarella stick into the air fryer basket. Cook at 400F for 10 minutes or until golden. Serve warm.

Bacon-Wrapped Onion Rings
Cook time: 10 minutes |Serves: 4 | Per serving: Calories 105; Carbs 3.7g; Fat 5.9g; Protein 7.5g

Ingredients:

- o   Large onion – 1, sliced into ¼ inch thick slices
- o   Sriracha – 1 tbsp.
- o   Bacon – 8 slices

Directions:

Brush sriracha over the onion slices. Take two slices of onion and wrap bacon around the rings. Repeat with the remaining onion and bacon. Place into the air fryer basket. Cook at 350F for 10 minutes. Flip the onion rings halfway through the cooking time. Serve warm.

Sweet Pepper Poppers
Cook time: 8 minutes |Serves: 4| Per serving: Calories 176; Carbs 2.7g; Fat 13.4g; Protein 7.4g

Ingredients:

- o   Mini sweet peppers – 8 (seeds and membranes removed)
- o   Full-fat cream cheese – 4 ounces, softened
- o   Bacon – 4 slices, cooked and crumbled
- o   Shredded pepper jack cheese – ¼ cup

Directions:

In a bowl, mix bacon, cream cheese, and pepper jack. Place 3 tsps. of the mixture into each sweet pepper and press down firmly. Place in the air fryer basket. Cook at 400F for 8 minutes. Serve warm.

Spicy Spinach Artichoke Dip

Cook time: 10 minutes |Serves: 6| Per serving: Calories 226; Carbs 6.5g; Fat 15.9g; Protein 10g

Ingredients:

- o Frozen spinach – 10 ounces, drained and thawed
- o Artichoke hearts – 1 (14-ounce) can, drained and chopped
- o Chopped pickled jalapenos – ¼ cup
- o Full-fat cream cheese – 8 ounces, softened
- o Full-fat sour cream – ¼ cup
- o Full-fat mayonnaise – ¼ cup
- o Garlic powder – ½ tsp.
- o Grated Parmesan cheese – ¼ cup
- o Shredded pepper jack cheese – 1 cup

Directions:

Mix all ingredients in a baking bowl. Place into the air fryer basket. Cook at 320F for 10 minutes. Serve warm.

Potato Wedges

Cook time: 25 minutes |Serves: 4 | Per serving: Calories 171; Carbs 18g; Fat 8g; Protein 7g

Ingredients:

- o Potatoes – 2, cut into wedges
- o Olive oil – 1 tbsp.
- o Salt and black pepper to taste
- o Sour cream – 3 tbsps.
- o Sweet chili sauce – 2 tbsps.

Directions:

In a bowl, mix potato wedges with oil, salt, and pepper. Toss well. Add to the air fryer basket and cook at 360F for 25 minutes. Flip once. Divide potato wedges onto plates. Drizzle chili sauce and sour cream all over and serve.

Mushroom Dish

Cook time: 8 minutes |Serves: 4| Per serving: Calories 241; Carbs 14g; Fat 7g; Protein 6g

Ingredients:

- o Button mushrooms – 10, stems removed
- o Italian seasoning – 1 tbsp.
- o Salt and black pepper to taste
- o Cheddar cheese – 2 tbsps. grated
- o Olive oil – 1 tbsp.
- o Mozzarella – 2 tbsps. grated
- o Dill – 1 tbsp. chopped

Directions:

In a bowl, mix mushrooms with oil, seasoning, dill, salt, and pepper. Mix well. Arrange mushrooms in your air fryer basket, sprinkle mozzarella and cheddar in each and cook them at 360F for 8 minutes. Divide them between plates and serve.

Sweet Potato Fries

Cook time: 20 minutes |Serves: 2| Per serving: Calories 200; Carbs 9g; Fat 5g; Protein 7g

Ingredients:

- o Sweet potatoes – 2, peeled and cut into medium fries
- o Salt and black pepper to taste
- o Olive oil – 2 tbsps.
- o Curry powder – ½ tsp.
- o Coriander – ¼ tsp. ground
- o Ketchup – ¼ cup
- o Mayonnaise – 2 tbsps.
- o Cumin – ½ tsp. ground
- o Ginger powder – 1 pinch

o   Cinnamon powder – 1 pinch

Directions:

In the air fryer's basket, mix sweet potato fries with salt, pepper, coriander, curry powder, and oil. Toss well. Cook at 370F for 20 minutes. Flipping once. Meanwhile, in a bowl, mix ketchup with cinnamon, ginger, cumin, and mayo. Whisk well. Divide fries on plates. Drizzle ketchup mix over them and serve.

Corn with Lime and Cheese
Cook time: 15 minutes |Serves: 2| Per serving: Calories 200; Carbs 6g; Fat 5g; Protein 6g

Ingredients:

o   Corns on the cob – 2, husks removed

o   A drizzle of olive oil

o   Feta cheese – ½ cup, grated

o   Sweet paprika – 2 tsps.

o   Juice from 2 limes

Directions:

Rub corn with oil and paprika. Place in the air fryer basket and cook at 400F for 15 minutes. Flip once. Divide corn on plates, sprinkle cheese on top. Drizzle with lime juice and serve.

Brussels Sprouts
Cook time: 15 minutes |Serves: 4| Per serving: Calories 172; Carbs 12g; Fat 6g; Protein 6g

Ingredients:

o   Brussels sprouts – 1 pound, trimmed and halved

o   Salt and black pepper to taste

o   Olive oil – 6 tsps.

o   Thyme – ½ tsp. chopped

o   Mayonnaise – ½ cup

o   Roasted garlic – 2 tbsps. crushed

Directions:

Mix Brussels sprouts with oil, salt and pepper in the air fryer basket and toss well. Cook them at 390F for 15 minutes. Meanwhile, in a bowl, mix mayo, thyme, and garlic and whisk well. Divide Brussels sprouts on plates, drizzle garlic sauce all over and serve.

Creamy Potato
Cook time: 1 hour 20 minutes |Serves: 2 | Per serving: Calories 172; Carbs 9g; Fat 5g; Protein 4g

Ingredients:

- o   Big potato – 1
- o   Bacon strips – 2, cooked and chopped
- o   Olive oil – 1 tsp.
- o   Cheddar cheese – 1/3 cup, shredded
- o   Green onions – 1 tbsp. chopped
- o   Salt and black pepper to taste
- o   Butter – 1 tbsp.
- o   Heavy cream – 2 tbsps.

Directions:

Rub potato with oil, season with salt and pepper. Place in the preheated air fryer and cook at 400F for 30 minutes. Flip potato, and cook for 30 minutes more. Transfer to a cutting board. Cool and slice in half lengthwise and scoop pulp in a bowl. Add salt, pepper, green onions, heavy cream, butter, cheese, and bacon. Stir well and stuff potato skins with this mix. Return potato to the air fryer and cook them at 400F for 20 minutes. Divide among plates and serve.

Green Beans
Cook time: 25 minutes |Serves: 4| Per serving: Calories 152; Carbs 7g; Fat 3g; Protein 4g

Ingredients:

- o   Green beans – 1 ½ pounds, trimmed and steamed for 2 minutes
- o   Salt and black pepper to taste
- o   Shallots – ½ pound, chopped
- o   Almonds – ¼ cup, toasted
- o   Olive oil – 2 tbsps.

Directions:

Mix green beans with oil, almonds, shallots, salt, and pepper in the air fryer basket. Toss well and cook at 400F for 25 minutes. Divide among plates and serve.

Parmesan Mushrooms

Cook time: 15 minutes |Serves: 3| Per serving: Calories 124; Carbs 7g; Fat 4g; Protein 3g

Ingredients:

- o Button mushroom caps – 9
- o Cream cracker slices – 3, crumbled
- o Egg white – 1
- o Parmesan – 2 tbsps. grated
- o Italian seasoning – 1 tsp.
- o Salt and black pepper
- o Butter – 1 tbsp. melted

Directions:

Mix crackers with butter, Parmesan, salt, pepper, seasoning, and egg white. Stir well and stuff mushrooms with this mix. Arrange mushrooms in the air fryer basket and cook them at 360F for 15 minutes. Divide among plates and serve.

Air Fried Eggplant

Cook time: 10 minutes |Serves: 4| Per serving: Calories 200; Carbs 12g; Fat 3g; Protein 4g

Ingredients:

- o Baby eggplants – 8, scooped in the center and pulp reserved
- o Salt and black pepper to taste
- o A pinch of oregano, dried
- o Green bell pepper – 1, chopped
- o Tomato paste – 1 tbsp.
- o Coriander – 1 bunch, chopped

- o   Garlic powder – ½ tsp.

- o   Olive oil – 1 tbsp.

- o   Yellow onion – 1, chopped

- o   Tomato – 1, chopped

Directions:

Heat oil in a pan and add the onion. Stir-fry for 1 minute. Add tomato, coriander, garlic powder, tomato paste, green bell pepper, oregano, eggplant pulp, salt, and pepper. Stir-fry for 2 minutes more. Remove from heat and cool. Stuff eggplants with this mix; place them in the air fryer's basket. Cook at 360F for 8 minutes. Divide eggplants between plates and serve.

Banana Cake

Cook time: 30 minutes |Serves: 4| Per serving: Calories 232; Carbs 34g; Fat 4g; Protein 4g

Ingredients:

- Soft butter – 1 tbsp.
- Egg – 1
- Brown sugar – 1/3 cup
- Honey – 2 tbsps.
- Banana – 1, peeled and mashed
- White flour – 1 cup
- Baking powder – 1 tsp.
- Cinnamon powder – ½ tsp.
- Cooking spray

Directions:

Spray a cake pan with cooking spray and set aside. In a bowl, mix flour, baking powder, cinnamon, egg, honey, banana, sugar, and butter. Whisk. Pour the batter into the greased cake pan and cook in the air fryer at 350F for 30 minutes. Cool, slice and serve.

Cheesecake

Cook time: 15 minutes |Serves: 15 | Per serving: Calories 245; Carbs 20g; Fat 12g; Protein 3g

Ingredients:

- Cream cheese – 1 pound

- o   Vanilla extract – ½ tsp.

- o   Eggs – 2

- o   Sugar – 4 tbsps.

- o   Graham crackers – 1 cup, crumbled

- o   Butter – 2 tbsps.

Directions:

Mix crackers with the butter in a bowl. Press crackers mix on the bottom of a lined cake pan. Place in the air fryer and cook at 350F for 4 minutes. Meanwhile, in a bowl, mix eggs, cream cheese, sugar, and vanilla and whisk well. Spread filling over crackers crust and cook in the air fryer at 310F for 15 minutes. Cool and keep in the refrigerator for 3 hours. Slice and serve.

Bread Pudding
Cook time: 1 hour |Serves: 4| Per serving: Calories 302; Carbs 23g; Fat 8g; Protein 10g

Ingredients:

- o   Glazed doughnuts – 6, crumbled

- o   Cherries – 1 cup

- o   Egg – 4 yolks

- o   Whipping cream – 1 ½ cups

- o   Raisins – ½ cup

- o   Sugar – ¼ cup

- o   Chocolate chips – ½ cup

Directions:

In a bowl, mix cherries, with egg yolks, and whipping cream and stir well. In another bowl, mix doughnuts, chocolate chips, sugar, and raisins. Mix. Combine 2 mixtures and transfer everything to a greased pan that fits in your air fryer and cook at 310F for 1 hour. Chill pudding before cutting and serve.

Cinnamon Rolls with Dip
Cook time: 15 minutes |Serves: 8| Per serving: Calories 200; Carbs 5g; Fat 1g; Protein 6g

Ingredients:

- o Bread dough – 1 pound

- o Brown sugar – ¾ cup

- o Cinnamon – 1 ½ tbsps. ground

- o Butter – ¼ cup, melted

For the cream cheese dip

- o Butter – 2 tbsps.

- o Cream cheese – 4 ounces

- o Sugar – 1 ¼ cups

- o Vanilla – ½ tsp.

Directions:

Roll dough on a floured working surface, shape a rectangle and brush with ¼ cup butter. Mix sugar and cinnamon in a bowl. Sprinkle this over the dough. Roll dough into a log. Seal well and cut into 8 pieces. Leave rolls to rise for 2 hours. Place them in the air fryer basket. Cook at 350F for 5 minutes. Then flip and cook 4 minutes more. Transfer to a platter. In a bowl, mix butter, cream cheese, sugar, and vanilla. Whisk well. Serve cinnamon rolls with this cream cheese dip.

Pumpkin Pie
Cook time: 15 minutes |Serves: 9| Per serving: Calories 200; Carbs 5g; Fat 5g; Protein 6g

Ingredients:

- o Sugar – 1 tbsp.

- o Flour – 2 tbsps.

- o Butter – 1 tbsp.

- o Water – 2 tbsps.

For the pumpkin pie filling

- o Pumpkin flesh – 3.5 ounces, chopped

- o Mixed spice – 1 tsp.

- o Nutmeg – 1 tsp.

- o Water – 3 ounces

- o   Egg – 1, whisked

- o   Sugar – 1 tbsp.

Directions:

Put 3 ounces of water in a pot. Bring to a boil and add pumpkin, 1 tbsp. of sugar, egg, spice, and nutmeg. Stir and boil for 20 minutes. Remove from the heat and blend with a hand mixer. In a bowl, mix butter, flour, 2 tbsps. of water, 1 tbsp. sugar and knead the dough well. Grease a pie pan with butter. Press dough into the pan. Fill with pumpkin pie filling. Place in the air fryer's basket and cook at 360F for 15 minutes. Serve.

Strawberry Donuts
Cook time: 15 minutes |Serves: 4| Per serving: Calories 250; Carbs 32g; Fat 12g; Protein 4g

Ingredients:

- o   Flour – 8 ounces

- o   Brown sugar – 1 tbsp.

- o   White sugar – 1 tbsp.

- o   Egg – 1

- o   Butter – 2 ½ tbsps.

- o   Whole milk – 4 ounces

- o   Baking powder – 1 tsp.

For the strawberry icing

- o   Butter – 2 tbsps.

- o   Icing sugar – 3.5 ounces

- o   Pink coloring – ½ tsp.

- o   Strawberries – ¼ cup, chopped

- o   Whipped cream – 1 tbsp.

Directions:

In a bowl, mix flour, 1 tbsp. white sugar, 1 tbsp. brown sugar, and butter and stir. In another bowl, mix the egg with 1 ½ tbsps. of butter and milk and stir well. Combine the 2 mixtures, stir, and shape donuts from this mix. Place them in the air fryer's basket and cook at 360F for 15 minutes. Put strawberry puree, whipped cream, food coloring, icing sugar, and 1 tbsp. butter and whisk well. Arrange the donuts on a platter and serve with strawberry icing on top.

Cocoa Cake

Cook time: 17 minutes |Serves: 6 | Per serving: Calories 340; Carbs 25g; Fat 11g; Protein 5g

Ingredients:

- Butter – 3.5 ounces, melted
- Eggs – 3
- Sugar – 3 ounces
- Cocoa powder – 1 tsp.
- Flour – 3 ounces
- Lemon juice – ½ tsp.

Directions:

In a bowl, mix cocoa powder, with 1 tbsp. butter and whisk. In another bowl, mix the rest of the butter with lemon juice, flour, eggs, and sugar. Whisk well and pour half into a cake pan. Add half of the cocoa mix, spread, add the rest of the butter layer and top with the rest of the cocoa. Cook in the air fryer at 360F for 17 minutes. Cool, sliced and serve.

Pumpkin Cake

Cook time: 30 minutes |Serves: 12| Per serving: Calories 232; Carbs 29g; Fat 7g; Protein 4g

Ingredients:

- White flour – ¾ cup
- Whole wheat flour – ¾ cup
- Baking soda – 1 tsp.
- Pumpkin pie spice – ¾ tsp.
- Sugar – ¾ cup
- Banana – 1, mashed
- Baking powder – ½ tsp.
- Canola oil – 2 tbsp.
- Greek yogurt – ½ cup

- o Canned pumpkin puree – 8 ounces

- o Cooking spray

- o Egg – 1

- o Vanilla extract – ½ tsp.

- o Chocolate chips – 2/3 cup

Directions:

In a bowl, mix whole wheat flour, white flour, salt, baking soda, baking powder, and pumpkin spice and stir. In another bowl, mix egg, vanilla, pumpkin puree, yogurt, banana, oil, and sugar. Mix with a mixer. Combine the 2 mixtures, and add the chocolate chips. Pour this into a greased Bundt pan. Place in the air fryer and cook at 330F for 30 minutes. Cool, slice and serve.

Apple Bread
Cook time: 40 minutes |Serves: 6| Per serving: Calories 192; Carbs 14g; Fat 6g; Protein 7g

Ingredients:

- o Apples – 3, cored and cubed

- o Sugar – 1 cup

- o Vanilla – 1 tbsp.

- o Eggs – 2

- o Apple pie spice – 1 tbsp.

- o White flour – 2 cups

- o Baking powder – 1 tbsp.

- o Butter – 1 stick

- o Water – 1 cup

Directions:

In a bowl, mix 1 stick butter, eggs, apple pie spice, and sugar and stir with a mixer. Add apples and stir well. In another bowl, mix flour and baking powder. Combine the 2 mixtures. Stir and pour into a springform pan. Put springform pan in the air fryer and cook at 320F for 40 minutes. Slice and serve.

Mini Lava Cakes

Cook time: 20 minutes |Serves: 3| Per serving: Calories 201; Carbs 23g; Fat 7g; Protein 4g

Ingredients:

- o Egg – 1
- o Sugar – 4 tbsps.
- o Olive oil – 2 tbsps.
- o Milk – 4 tbsps.
- o Flour – 4 tbsps.
- o Cocoa powder – 1 tbsp.
- o Baking powder – ½ tsp.
- o Orange zest – ½ tsp.

Directions:

In a bowl, mix oil, sugar, milk, egg, flour, salt, cocoa powder, baking powder, and orange zest. Mix well and pour into greased ramekins. Add ramekins to the air fryer and cook at 320F for 20 minutes. Serve.

Carrot Cake

Cook time: 45 minutes |Serves: 6| Per serving: Calories 200; Carbs 22g; Fat 6g; Protein 4g

Ingredients:

- o Flour – 5 ounces
- o Baking powder – ¾ tsp.
- o Baking soda – ½ tsp.
- o Cinnamon powder – ½ tsp.
- o Allspice - ½ tsp.
- o Nutmeg – ¼ tsp. ground
- o Egg – 1
- o Yogurt – 3 tbsps.
- o Sugar – ½ cup

- o Pineapple juice – ¼ cup

- o Sunflower oil – 4 tbsps.

- o Carrots – 1/3 cup, grated

- o Pecans – 1/3 cup, toasted and chopped

- o Coconut flakes – 1/3 cup, shredded

- o Cooking spray

Directions:

In a bowl, mix flour, nutmeg, cinnamon, allspice, salt, baking soda, and powder and mix. In another bowl, mix the egg with coconut flakes, pecans, carrots, oil, pineapple juice, sugar, and yogurt. Combine the two mixtures and mix well. Pour this into a greased springform pan. Place the pan in the air fryer and cook at 320F for 45 minutes. Cool, slice and serve.

Ginger Cheesecake
Cook time: 20 minutes |Serves: 6| Per serving: Calories 412; Carbs 20g; Fat 12g; Protein 6g

Ingredients:

- o Butter – 2 tsps. melted

- o Ginger cookies – ½ cup, crumbled

- o Cream cheese – 16 ounces, soft

- o Eggs – 2

- o Sugar – ½ cup

- o Rum – 1 tsp.

- o Vanilla extract – ½ tsp.

- o Nutmeg – ½ tsp. ground

Directions:

Grease a pan with butter and spread cookie crumbs on the bottom. In a bowl, beat cream cheese, eggs, rum, vanilla, and nutmeg. Whisk well and spread over the cookie crumbs. Place in the air fryer and cook at 340F for 20 minutes. Cool and keep in the refrigerator. Slice and serve.

Strawberry Pie

Cook time: 20 minutes |Serves: 12 | Per serving: Calories 234; Carbs 6g; Fat 23g; Protein 7g

Ingredients for the crust

- o Coconut – 1 cup, shredded
- o Sunflower seeds – 1 cup
- o Butter – ¼ cup

For the filling

- o Gelatin – 1 tsp.
- o Cream cheese – 8 ounces
- o Strawberries – 4 ounces
- o Water – 2 tbsps.
- o Lemon juice – ½ tbsp.
- o Stevia – ¼ tsp.
- o Heavy cream – ½ cup
- o Strawberries – 8 ounces, chopped for serving

Directions:

Mix sunflower seeds, coconut, butter, and salt in a food processor. Pulse and press the mixture on the bottom of a cake pan. Heat up a pan with the water over medium heat. Add gelatin, and stir until it dissolves. Set aside to cool down. Add the gelatin mixture, 4 ounces strawberries, lemon juice, cream cheese, and stevia in a food processor and blend well. Add heavy cream, stir well and spread over crust. Top with 8 ounces strawberries. Place in the air fryer and cook at 330F for 15 minutes. Keep in the fridge until you serve it.

Coffee Cheesecake

Cook time: 20 minutes |Serves: 6| Per serving: Calories 254; Carbs 21g; Fat 23g; Protein 5g

Ingredients for the cheesecakes

- o Butter – 2 tbsps.
- o Cream cheese – 8 ounces
- o Coffee – 3 tbsps.

- o Eggs – 3
- o Sugar – 1/3 cup
- o Caramel syrup - 1 tbsp.

For the frosting

- o Caramel syrup – 3 tbsps.
- o Butter – 3 tbsps.
- o Mascarpone cheese – 8 ounces, soft
- o Sugar – 2 tbsps.

Directions:

In the blender, mix eggs, cream cheese, 1/3 cup sugar, 1 tbsp. caramel syrup, coffee, and 2 tbsps. butter. Pulse very well and spoon into a cupcake pan. Cook in the air fryer at 320F for 20 minutes. Cool and keep in the freezer for 3 hours. Meanwhile, in a bowl, mix mascarpone, 2 tbsps. sugar, 3 tbsps. caramel syrup, and 3 tbsps. butter. Blend well and spoon over cheesecakes and serve them.

Special Brownies
Cook time: 17 minutes |Serves: 4| Per serving: Calories 223; Carbs 3g; Fat 32g; Protein 6g

Ingredients:

- o Egg – 1
- o Cocoa powder – 1/3 cup
- o Sugar – 1/3 cup
- o Butter – 7 tbsps.
- o Vanilla extract – ½ tsp.
- o White flour – ¼ cup
- o Walnuts – ¼ cup, chopped
- o Baking powder – ½ tsp.
- o Peanut butter – 1 tbsp.

Directions:

Add 6 tbsps. butter and sugar in a pan and heat over medium heat. Stir and cook for 5 minutes. Transfer to a bowl. Add flour, walnuts, baking powder, egg, cocoa powder, vanilla extract, and salt. Mix well and pour into a pan. In a bowl, mix peanut butter and 1 tbsp. butter. Heat up in the microwave for a few seconds. Mix well and drizzle over brownie mix. Place the pan in the air fryer and bake at 320F for 17 minutes. Cool, cut and serve.

Almond Butter Cookie Balls
Cook time: 10 minutes |Serves: 10| Per serving: Calories 224; Carbs 1.3g; Fat 16g; Protein 11.2g

Ingredients:

- Almond butter – 1 cup

- Egg - 1

- Vanilla extract – 1 tsp.

- Low carb protein powder – ¼ cup

- Powdered erythritol – ¼ cup

- Unsweetened coconut – ¼ cup, shredded

- Chocolate chips – ¼ cup

- Ground cinnamon – ½ tsp.

Directions:

Mix egg and almond butter in a bowl. Add erythritol, protein powder, and vanilla. Fold in cinnamon, chocolate chips, and coconut. Roll into 1-inch balls. Place balls into a baking pan and put into the air fryer basket. Cook at 320F for 10 minutes. Cool and serve.

Pecan Brownies
Cook time: 20 minutes |Serves: 6| Per serving: Calories 215; Carbs 2.3g; Fat 18.9g; Protein 4.2g

Ingredients:

- Almond flour – ½ cup

- Powdered erythritol – ½ cup

- Unsweetened cocoa powder – 2 tbsps.

- Baking powder – ½ tsp.

- Unsalted butter – ¼ cup, softened

- o   Egg – 1

- o   Chopped pecans – ¼ cup

- o   Chocolate chips – ¼ cup

Directions:

Mix almond flour, baking powder, cocoa powder, and erythritol in a bowl. Stir in egg and butter. Fold in chocolate chips and pecans. Scoop mixture into a baking pan and place the pan into the air fryer basket. Cook at 300F for 20 minutes. Cool, sliced and serve.

Mini Cheesecake

Cook time: 15 minutes |Serves: 2| Per serving: Calories 531; Carbs 5.1g; Fat 48.3g; Protein 11.4g

Ingredients:

- o   Walnuts – ½ cup

- o   Salted butter – 2 tbsps.

- o   Granular erythritol – 2 tbsps.

- o   Full-fat cream cheese – 4 ounces, softened

- o   Egg – 1

- o   Vanilla extract – ½ tsp.

- o   Powdered erythritol – 1/8 cup

Directions:

Place granular erythritol, butter, and walnuts in a food processor. Pulse until a dough forms. Press dough into a 4-inch springform pan and place the pan into the air fryer basket. Cook at 400F for 5 minutes. Remove, and cool. In a bowl, mix egg, cream cheese, powdered erythritol, and vanilla extract until smooth. Spoon mixture on top of baked walnut crust and place into the air fryer basket. Cook at 300F for 10 minutes. Chill for 2 hours and serve.

Mini Chocolate Chip Pan Cookie

Cook time: 7 minutes |Serves: 4| Per serving: Calories 188; Carbs 2.3g; Fat 15.7g; Protein 5.6g

Ingredients:

- o   Almond flour – ½ cup

- o   Powdered erythritol – ¼ cup

- o Unsalted butter – 2 tbsps. softened

- o Egg – 1

- o Unflavored gelatin – ½ tsp.

- o Baking powder – ½ tsp.

- o Vanilla extract – ½ tsp.

- o Chocolate chips – 2 tbsps.

Directions:

Mix almond and erythritol in a bowl. Stir in gelatin, egg, and butter. Mix until combined. Stir in vanilla and baking powder and then fold in chocolate chips. Pour batter into a round baking pan and place the pan into the air fryer basket. Cook at 300F for 7 minutes. Cool and serve.

Chocolate Chip Cookie
Cook time: 9 minutes |Serves: 4| Per serving: Calories 347; Carbs 3.8g; Fat 30.9g; Protein 8.3g

Ingredients:

- o Almond flour – ½ cup

- o Powdered erythritol – 1 cup, divided

- o Unsweetened cocoa powder – 2 tbsps.

- o Baking powder – ½ tsp.

- o Unsalted butter – ¼ cup, softened

- o Eggs – 2, divided

- o Full-fat cream cheese – 8 ounces, softened

- o Heavy whipping cream – ¼ cup

- o Vanilla extract – 1 tsp.

- o Peanut butter – 2 tbsps.

Directions:

In a bowl, mix ½ cup erythritol, almond flour, baking powder, and cocoa powder. Stir in one egg and butter. Scoop mixture into a 6-inch round baking pan. Place pan into the air fryer basket. Cook at 300F for 20 minutes. In a bowl, beat remaining ½-cup erythritol, cream cheese, heavy cream, peanut butter, vanilla, and remaining egg until fluffy. Pour mixture over cooled brownies. Place pan back into the air fryer basket. Cook at 300F for 15 minutes. Cool, then refrigerate for 2 hours before serving.

Mug Cake
Cook time: 25 minutes |Serves: 1| Per serving: Calories 237; Carbs 5.7g; Fat 16.4g; Protein 9.9g

Ingredients:

- o   Egg – 1
- o   Coconut flour – 2 tbsps.
- o   Heavy whipping cream – 2 tbsps.
- o   Granular erythritol – 2 tbsps.
- o   Vanilla extract – ¼ tsp.
- o   Baking powder – ¼ tsp.

Directions:

Whisk egg in a 4-inch ramekin. Then add the remaining ingredients and mix. Stir until smooth. Place into the air fryer basket.   Cook at 300F for 25 minutes. Serve.

Pound Cake
Cook time: 25 minutes |Serves: 6| Per serving: Calories 253; Carbs 3.2g; Fat 22.6g; Protein 6.9g

Ingredients:

- o   Almond flour – 1 cup
- o   Salted butter – ¼ cup, melted
- o   Granular erythritol – ½ cup
- o   Vanilla extract – 1 tsp.
- o   Baking powder – 1 tsp.
- o   Full-fat sour cream – ½ cup
- o   Full-fat cream cheese – 1 ounce, softened
- o   Eggs – 2

Directions:

Mix erythritol, butter, and flour in a bowl. Add in cream cheese, sour cream, baking powder, and vanilla. Mix well. Add eggs and mix. Pour batter into a 6-inch round baking pan. Place the pan into the air fryer basket. Cook at 300F for 25 minutes. Cool and serve.

Chocolate Mayo Cake

Cook time: 25 minutes |Serves: 6| Per serving: Calories 270; Carbs 3g; Fat 25g; Protein 7g

Ingredients:

- o Almond flour – 1 cup
- o Salted butter – ¼ cup, melted
- o Granular erythritol – ½ cup, plus 1 tbsp.
- o Vanilla extract – 1 tsp.
- o Full-fat mayonnaise – ¼ cup
- o Unsweetened cocoa powder – ¼ cup
- o Eggs – 2

Directions:

Mix all the ingredients in a bowl until smooth. Pour batter into a round baking pan. Place the pan into the air fryer basket. Cook at 300F for 25 minutes. Cool and serve.

Raspberry Danish Bites

Cook time: 7 minutes |Serves: 10| Per serving: Calories 96; Carbs 4g; Fat 7.7g; Protein 3.4g

Ingredients:

- o Almond flour – 1 cup
- o Baking powder – 1 tsp.
- o Granular swerve – 3 tbsps.
- o Full-fat cream cheese – 2 ounces, softened
- o Egg – 1
- o Raspberry preserve – 10 tsps.

Directions:

Mix all ingredients except preserve in a bowl and make a dough. Place the bowl in the freezer for 20 minutes, then roll it to make 10 balls. Press gently in the center of each ball. Place 1 tsp. preserves in the center of each ball. Line the air fryer basket with parchment. Place each Danish bite on the parchment. Press down gently to flatten the bottom. Cook at 400F for 7 minutes. Cool and serve.

Peanut Butter Cookies

Cook time: 8 minutes | Serves: 8 | Per serving: Calories 210; Carbs 2.1g; Fat 17.5g; Protein 8.8g

Ingredients:

- o   Smooth peanut butter – 1 cup
- o   Granular erythritol – 1/3 cup
- o   Egg – 1
- o   Vanilla extract – 1 tsp.

Directions:

Mix all the ingredients in a bowl until smooth. Continue to stir until the mixture begins to thicken. Roll the mixture into eight balls and press gently down to flatten into 2-inch round disks. Line the air fryer basket with parchment. Place the cookies onto the parchment. Work in batches if necessary. Cook at 320F for 8 minutes. Flip the cookies at the 6-minute mark. Serve.

Cinnamon Cream Puffs

Cook time: 6 minutes | Serves: 8 | Per serving: Calories 178; Carbs 1.3; Fat 12.1g; Protein 14.9g

Ingredients:

- o   Almond flour – ½ cup
- o   Vanilla protein powder – ½ cup
- o   Granular erythritol – ½ cup
- o   Baking powder – ½ tsp.
- o   Egg – 1
- o   Unsalted butter – 5 tbsps. melted
- o   Full-fat cream cheese – 2 ounces
- o   Powdered erythritol – ¼ tsp.

- o   Ground cinnamon – ¼ tsp.

- o   Heavy whipping cream – 2 tbsps.

- o   Vanilla extract – ½ tsp.

Directions:

Mix butter, egg, baking powder, granular erythritol, protein powder, and flour in a bowl to make a dough. Keep the dough in the freezer for 20 minutes. Roll the dough with wet hands to make eight balls. Line the air fryer basket with parchment. Place the dough balls into the air fryer basket. Cook at 380F for 6 minutes. Flip halfway through the cooking time. Remove and cool the puffs. In a bowl, beat cream, cream cheese, powdered erythritol, cinnamon, and vanilla until fluffy. Cut a small hole in the bottom of each puff and fill with some of the cream mixtures. Serve.

Molten Lava Cakes
Cook time: 12 minutes |Serves: 4| Per serving: Calories 360; Carbs 19g; Fat 29g; Protein 5.2g

Ingredients:

- o   Self-raising flour – 1.5 tbsps.

- o   Baker's sugar – 3.5 tbsps.

- o   Unsalted butter – 3.5 oz.

- o   Dark chocolate – 3.5 oz. chopped

- o   Eggs – 2

Directions:

Preheat the air fryer to 375F. Grease and flour 4 ramekins. Melt butter and dark chocolate in the microwave. Stirring throughout. Mix sugar and egg until frothy and pale. Pour melted chocolate mixture into the egg mixture. Stir in flour and mix everything. Fill the ramekins about ¾ full with batter. Bake in the air fryer at 375F for 10 minutes. Remove, cool and serve.

Chocolate Cake II
Cook time: 30 minutes |Serves: 6| Per serving: Calories 385.5; Carbs 42g; Fat 22g; Protein 6.8g

Ingredients:

- o   Eggs – 3

- o   Sour cream – ½ cup

- o   Flour – 1 cup

- o   Sugar – 2/3 cup

- o   Butter – 1 stick, room temperature

- o   Cocoa powder – 1/3 cup

- o   Baking powder – 1 tsp.

- o   Baking soda – ½ tsp.

- o   Vanilla – 2 tsps.

Directions:

Preheat air fryer to 320F. Mix the wet ingredients in a bowl and dry ingredients in another. Gradually pour the dry mixture into the wet. Lightly mix. Place in the air fryer basket. Cook for 25 minutes. Check if the cake is done, if not then cook for another 5 more minutes. Cool on a wire rack.

Cheesecake Bites
Cook time: 7 minutes |Serves: 2| Per serving: Calories 110; Carbs 1g; Fat 7g; Protein 2g

Ingredients:

- o   Cream cheese – 8 oz. softened

- o   Erythritol – ½ cup, plus 2 tbsps.

- o   Vanilla extract – ½ tsp.

- o   Almond flour – ½ cup

- o   Heavy cream – ½ packet

Directions:

Mix the cream cheese with ½ packet heavy cream, ½-cup erythritol, and vanilla extract until smooth. Scoop the mixture onto a parchment paper-lined baking sheet. Freeze for 30 minutes for the best results. Mix the almond flour with 2 tbsps. of erythritol in a bowl. Roll the frozen bites into the almond flour mixture. Place the cheesecake bites into the air fryer basket and cook for 7 minutes at 370F.

Brownies
Cook time: 20 minutes |Serves: 6| Per serving: Calories 215; Carbs 2.3g; Fat 18.9g; Protein 4.2g

Ingredients:

- o Almond flour – ½ cup

- o Powdered erythritol – ½ cup

- o Unsweetened cocoa powder – 2 tbsps.

- o Baking powder – ½ tsp.

- o Unsalted butter – ¼ cup, softened

- o Egg – 1

- o Chopped pecans – ¼ cup

- o Chocolate chips – ¼ cup

Directions:

Mix almond flour, baking powder, cocoa powder, and erythritol in a bowl. Stir in egg and butter. Fold in chocolate chips and pecans. Scoop mixture into a baking pan and place the pan into the air fryer basket. Cook at 300F for 20 minutes. Cool, slice and serve.

Chocolate Chip Cookie

Cook time: 9 minutes |Serves: 4| Per serving: Calories 362; Carbs 4g; Fat 27.3g; Protein 6g

Ingredients:

- o Softened butter – 3 tbsps.

- o Erythritol – ¼ cup plus 1 tbsp. powdered

- o Egg yolk – 1

- o Almond flour – ½ cup

- o Ground white chocolate – 2 tbsps. no sugar added

- o Baking soda – ¼ tsp.

- o Vanilla – ½ tsp.

- o Chocolate chips – ¾ cup, no sugar added

Directions:

In a medium bowl, beat the butter and erythritol together until fluffy. Stir in egg yolk. Add the vanilla, baking soda, white chocolate, and flour. Mix well. Stir in the chocolate chips. Line a baking pan with the parchment paper. Spray the parchment paper with nonstick baking spray. Spread the batter into the prepared pan, leaving a ½-inch border on all sides. Bake at 300F for 9 minutes or until cookie is lightly brown and just barely set. Remove the pan from the air fryer and let cook for 10 minutes. Remove the cookie from the pan, remove the parchment paper and let cool on a wire rack.

Marble Cake

Cook time: 17 minutes |Serves: 6| Per serving: Calories 277; Carbs 3.5g; Fat 27.9g; Protein 5.9g

Ingredients:

- o Erythritol - 7 tbsps. powdered
- o Almond flour – ½ cup
- o Eggs – 4, whisked
- o Baking powder – 1 tsp.
- o Cocoa powder – 5 tsps.
- o Butter – 2/3 cup, melted
- o Lime juice – ½ tsp.

Directions:

Preheat the air fryer to 356F. Mix 3 tbsp. of melted butter with the cocoa powder to form a paste. Add the erythritol to the remaining butter and mix well. Stir in the eggs, almond flour, and baking powder and mix until smooth. Pour in the lime and stir. Place a greased baking pan into the air fryer and allow to heat for a minute. Pour some of the batter into the hot pan then add a layer of the chocolate mixture, then the batter, chocolate and lastly top with batter. Use a skewer to create a swirl. Place in the air fryer and bake for 17 minutes.

Chocolate Cake

Cook time: 25 minutes |Serves: 6| Per serving: Calories 321; Carbs 7.2g; Fat 30.8g; Protein 7.7g

Ingredients:

- o Eggs – 3
- o Sour cream – ½ cup
- o Almond flour – 1 cup
- o Erythritol – 2/3 cup, powdered
- o Butter – 1 stick, room temperature

- ○ Cocoa powder – 1/3 cup

- ○ Baking powder – 1 tsp.

- ○ Baking soda – ½ tsp.

- ○ Vanilla – 2 tsps.

Directions:

Preheat air fryer to 320F. Mix the wet ingredients in a bowl and dry ingredients in another. Gradually pour the dry mixture into the wet. Lightly mix. Place in the air fryer basket. Cook for 25 minutes. Check if the cake is done, if not then cook for another 5 more minutes. Cool on a wire rack.

Lemon Tarts
Cook time: 15 minutes |Serves: 4| Per serving: Calories 304; Carbs 8.6g; Fat 29.9g; Protein 2.9g

Ingredients:

- ○ Butter – ½ cup

- ○ Almond flour – ½ pound

- ○ Erythritol – 3 tbsps. powdered

- ○ Lemon – 1 large (juice and zest)

- ○ Lemon curd – 2 tbsps.

- ○ Nutmeg – 1 pinch

Directions:

In a bowl, combine erythritol, almond flour, and butter. Mix until looks like breadcrumbs. Then add lemon zest and juice, and cinnamon and mix again. If needed, add 2 tbsps. of water to make a soft dough. Sprinkle pastry tins with almond flour. Add dough and top with lemon curd. Preheat the air fryer to 360F and cook mini lemon tarts for 15 minutes or until ready. Serve.

Coconut Cookies
Cook time: 12 minutes |Serves: 10 | Per serving: Calories 206; Carbs 6.7g; Fat 18g; Protein 4.8g

Ingredients:

- ○ Egg – 1

- ○ Dried coconut – 3 tbsps.

155

- Butter – 3 oz.

- Erythritol – 2 oz. powdered

- Vanilla extract – 1 tsp.

- Chocolate – 2 oz. no sugar added

- Almond flour – 5 oz.

Directions:

In a bowl, beat butter and erythritol until fluffy. Add one egg, vanilla extract and stir to combine. Crush the chocolate into small pieces. Add them to the mixture. Roll small balls with hands. Roll these balls in the dried coconut. Place balls on the baking sheet. Preheat the air fryer to 370F. Bake coconut balls for 8 minutes. Shake once. Lower temperature to 280 to 300F and cook for 4 minutes more. Serve.

Conclusion

The Instant Pot air fryer crisp has made cooking and living easier for every cooking enthusiast. With this cooking appliance, you have a variety of cooking options such as sauté, steam, pressure cook, slow cook, warm, air fry, bake, roast, broil, and more! The quick and smart program makes this appliance easy for everyone to use it, from a naïve cook to a professional chef. With almost everything done with the touch of your fingertip, you will no longer be a slave to your kitchen and cooking tasks. Also, clean-up tasks will no longer be as time-consuming as they used to be for any housewife or cook.

Made in the USA
Middletown, DE
10 August 2020